CHILDREN'S ENCYCLOPEDIA OF THE SOLAR SYSTEM

Claudia Martin

ARCTURUS

Picture Credits:
Alamy: 4-5 (Ollie Taylor), 8-9, 66-67 (Mark Garlick/Science Photo Library), 14-15 (Ron Miller/Stocktrek Images), 38-39 (NASA Images), 68cl (Alan Dyer/Stocktrek Images), 70-71 (Walter Myers/Stocktrek Images), 78c (Encyclopedia Britannica/Universal Images Group North America), 82cr (World History Archive), 102-103 (NASA Photo), 112-113 (World History Archive), 118br (QAI Publishing/Universal Images Group), 124-125 (NASA/RGB Ventures/Superstock), 125cr (BJ Warnick/Newscom); **Areong:** 60bc (NASA); **China News Service:** 116cr; **ESA:** 60cr (DLR/ FU Berlin/J. Cowart), 88cr (2010 MPS for OSIRIS Team MPS/UPD/LAM/IAA/RSSD/INTA/UPM/DASP/IDA); **Getty Images:** 6-7 (QAI Publishing/ Universal Images Group), 113tl (China National Space Administration/AFP), 114-115 (Adrian Mann/All About Space Magazine); **Matúš Motlo:** 12bl; **NASA:** 10c (ESA, N. Smith [University of California, Berkeley], and The Hubble Heritage Team [STScI/AURA]; credit for CTIO Image: N. Smith [University of California, Berkeley] and NOAO/AURA/NSF), 14bl (NASA Goddard Laboratory for Atmospheres and Yohkoh Legacy Data Archive), 19t, 76c (NASA Goddard Space Flight Center, Greenbelt, MD, USA), 19cr (TRACE), 19br (NASA Goddard Photo and Video), 22br, 85b (Hubble Space Telescope), 38bl (GSFC/Arizona State University), 48bl, 50cr, 51tc (Johns Hopkins University Applied Physics Laboratory/ Carnegie Institution of Washington), 53b, 56-57, 56cr, 57c, 74cr, 82bl, 120br (JPL), 53tr, 117br (JPL-Caltech), 57br (JPL/Magellan Probe), 58cl (JPL-Caltech/MSSS), 58br (Viking 1), 60br (JPL/Malin Space Science Systems), 62cr (JPL-Caltech/Arizona State University), 62bl (World Wind), 64c (JPL-Caltech/University of Arizona), 64cr (JPL/University of Arizona), 68br (JPL-Caltech/Kevin M. Gill), 72cr (JPL-Caltech/SSI), 72bl (ESA, J. Clarke [Boston University], and Z. Levay [STScI]), 77br (JPL/Space Science Institute), 79bc (ESA and M. Showalter [SETI Institute]), 80cr (Erich Karkoschka, University of Arizona), 85cr (Voyager 2), 88cl (NEAR), 88c (USGS/JPL), 89bc (JPL/Processed by Kevin M. Gill), 90bl (JPL-Caltech/ UCLA/MPS/DLR/IDA), 96c (ESA and M. Brown), 102bl, 108bt, 112bl, 112bc, 112br, 122br, 124br (NASA Images), 110cr (National Archives at College Park), 114cl (Johns Hopkins APL/Steve Gribben), 117cr (John Frassanito & Associates), 122cr (ESA/JPL/University of Arizona; processed by Andrey Pivovarov), 123bc (JPL/NOAO/Jason Perry); **NSO/NSF/AURA:** 14cr; **Science Photo Library:** 5tr, 26br, 54-55, 60-61, 80-81, 87 (Mark Garlick), 6cl (Paul D Stewart), 22-23 (Paul Wootton), 24-25, 46-47, 54cl (NASA/Johns Hopkins University Applied Physics Laboratory/Carnegie Institution of Washington), 52c (Juan Carlos Casado/StarryEarth.com), 54br (Lynette Cook), 62-63 (Walter Myers), 84-85 (Ron Miller), 86cr (NASA/JPL-Caltech), 92-93 (NASA/Johns Hopkins University Applied Physics Laboratory/Southwest Research Institute/Steve Gribben), 96-97 (M. Brown/ CIT/NASA/ESA/STSCI), 96bl (Adam Nieman), 98cl (Jerry Lodriguss), 98br (Tim Brown), 100-101 (Jeff Dai), 102, 111tc, 120cl (NASA), 104-105 (NASA/JPL-Caltech/R. Hurt [SSC]), 104r (NASA/JPL), 106-107 (European Space Agency), 107r, 122-123 (David Ducros), 114br (ESA & NASA/Solar Orbiter/Spice Team), 118-119 (Julian Baum), 124c (Gregoire Cirade); **Shutterstock:** 1 (Vadim Sadovski), 4bl (Angel Soler Gollonet), 7tc, 110br (Nerthuz/NASA), 7tcr (NASA Images), 7tr, 70c (Tristan 3D), 8cr (John Erickson), 8bl (Marc Ward), 9br, 12cr, 31tr, 44cr, 46b, 67b (Designua), 10-11 (Mopic), 10br (D1min), 11r (Erebor Mountain), 12-13 (Valentin Valkov), 13br (Azuzl), 16-17 (Bo Valentino), 16l, 34br, 108cr (VectorMine), 17c (Aldona Griskeviciene), 17bl (Fouad A. Saad), 18cr (designer_an), 20-21 (Thanakrit Santikunaporn), 20ct (jflin98), 20cb (joelamfotohk), 20bl (Natursports), 21br, 44br (Alhovik), 22tl (sevenwe), 24b (Veronika By), 25bl (Redpixel.pl), 28-29, 68-69, 82-83, 94-95 (24K-Production/NASA), 28c, 30br, 105bc (Naeblys), 28br (Jane Kelly), 29bc (aphotostory), 30-31 (Fotos593), 30c (tinkivinki), 32-33 (Kedardome), 32c (shooarts), 33bc (Brian Donovan), 34-35 (ArCaLu), 34c (AnnSky), 35tr (Nicolas Primola), 36c, 38cr (Siberian Art), 37bc (PhotoVisions), 39br, 70br, 77tr, 80br (Blue bee), 40-41 (Pe3K/NASA), 42-43 (Soloviova Liudmyla), 42c (Inkoly), 43bl (Anna L. e Marina Durante), 44-45 (shuttertim82), 44c (mailbocy), 45tc (Aristokrates), 47tr (alexaldo), 49tr, 52br, 59br, 69br, 78br, 84br, 91br (Anatolir), 55br (Meggi), 58-59 (sakdam/NASA), 64-65, 120-121, 121cr (Dotted Yeti/NASA), 64br, 65tr (Kirius_Sirius), 66br (Whitelion61/NASA), 71br (ManuMata), 72-73 (3000ad/NASA), 73br, 83br (Golden Sikorka), 74-75 (bluecrayola), 75tc (Artsiom P/NASA), 75cr (Elena11/NASA), 76-77 (Stephane Masclaux), 78-79 (buradaki/NASA), 81cr, 92bl (Diego Barucco), 86bl (Claudio Caridi), 86bc (Meletios Verras), 88-89 (3d_vicka), 90-91 (Nostalgia for Infinity/NASA), 90cr (Marc Ward/NASA), 92cr (Lukas Bischoff Photograph), 94c (Vector Point Studio), 94br (gomolach), 95tr (Anna Sizova), 98-99 (Diego Hartog Rebello), 100cr (R G Meier), 100br (Marina_Maximova), 101bc (marcin jucha), 103tr (grimgram), 104br (ioanna_alexa), 108-109 (Vadim Sadovski/NASA), 108cl (Sergey Merkulov), 108bc (Mechanik), 108bb (bluebay), 109br (3DMI), 110-111, 118cl (3Dsculptor/NASA), 113br (RikoBest), 115tr (Alex Terentii), 116-117 (Merlin74/NASA), 119bc (Raymond Cassel). Front cover: main image Getty (adventtr), small images L Shutterstock (BEST-BACKGROUNDS), CL Shutterstock (agpotterphoto), C NASA, CR Shutterstock (Elena11), R Shutterstock (tuntekron petsajun). Back cover: Shutterstock titoOnz. Front flap: NASA. Back flap: Shutterstock IgorZh.

ARCTURUS

This edition published in 2023 by Arcturus Publishing Limited
26/27 Bickels Yard, 151–153 Bermondsey Street,
London SE1 3HA

ISBN: 978-1-3988-2587-1
CH010980US
Supplier 29, Date 0723, Print run 00003532

Author: Claudia Martin
Designer: Lorraine Inglis
Consultant: Dr. Helen Giles
Editor: Becca Clunes
Additional design: Gina Wood
Managing editor: Joe Harris

Printed in China

CONTENTS

Introduction

The Solar System is all the objects—from giant planets to small rocks—that are spinning around our star, the Sun. The Sun is one of 100 to 400 billion stars in our galaxy, the Milky Way. The Milky Way is one of perhaps 2 trillion galaxies in the Universe, which contains everything we know to exist.

During its journey around the Sun, the planet Mars ranges between 57.6 million and 400 million km (35.8 million and 249.1 million miles) from Earth.

The Moon is Earth's closest companion, at an average distance of 384,400 km (238,855 miles).

Not Alone

A solar system is a group of planets and smaller objects revolving around a star. Until 1992, ours was the only solar system we knew about. Then astronomers found an exoplanet, a planet revolving around a different star. Since then, more than 5,000 exoplanets have been spotted. Astronomers think there could be 100 billion solar systems in the Milky Way—and perhaps 1 septillion (1 followed by 24 zeros) in the Universe.

The Trappist-1 solar system is around 380 trillion km (236 trillion miles) away. Seven exoplanets are revolving around the Trappist-1 star.

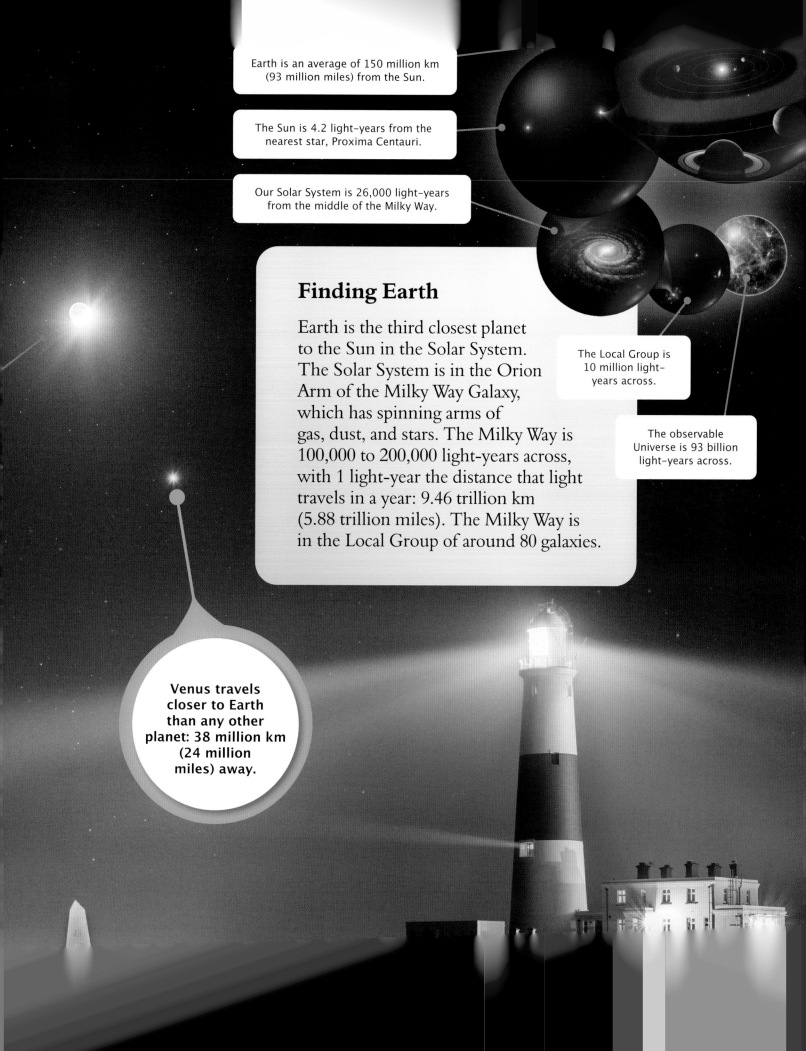

Earth is an average of 150 million km (93 million miles) from the Sun.

The Sun is 4.2 light-years from the nearest star, Proxima Centauri.

Our Solar System is 26,000 light-years from the middle of the Milky Way.

Finding Earth

Earth is the third closest planet to the Sun in the Solar System. The Solar System is in the Orion Arm of the Milky Way Galaxy, which has spinning arms of gas, dust, and stars. The Milky Way is 100,000 to 200,000 light-years across, with 1 light-year the distance that light travels in a year: 9.46 trillion km (5.88 trillion miles). The Milky Way is in the Local Group of around 80 galaxies.

The Local Group is 10 million light-years across.

The observable Universe is 93 billion light-years across.

Venus travels closer to Earth than any other planet: 38 million km (24 million miles) away.

Chapter 1

The Solar System

Eight planets, several smaller dwarf planets, and countless even smaller rocky, metal, and icy objects are orbiting (revolving around) the Sun. Six of the planets—as well as many dwarf planets and smaller objects—are themselves orbited by objects known as moons.

The Pull of Gravity

Gravity is a force that pulls all objects toward each other. The more massive the object, the stronger the pull of its gravity. The Sun's mass (weight) makes up 99.8 percent of the Solar System's mass. Its gravity is so immense that it holds the other Solar System objects in orbit.

English scientist Isaac Newton (1643–1727) figured out that the force that makes an apple fall from its branch to Earth is the same force that keeps the planets in their orbits.

The planets and most other Solar System objects travel in the same direction that the Sun is rotating: counterclockwise (anticlockwise) as seen from above Earth's north pole.

Uranus

The eight planets travel in roughly circular paths around the Sun's equator, all moving in the same plane, since they all formed from the same spinning disk of gas and dust.

DID YOU KNOW? The Sun's gravity is 28 times more powerful than Earth's gravity, so if you could stand on the Sun's surface, you would feel 28 times heavier than on Earth.

Planets, Dwarfs, and Moons

A planet is a large, rounded space object that orbits a star. Unlike a star, a planet does not produce its own light. A planet is massive enough for its gravity to have pulled it into a ball. Its gravity is also strong enough to clear other large objects out of its orbit. A dwarf planet orbits a star and is massive enough to be rounded, but it is not massive enough to clear its orbit. A moon may be bigger than a dwarf planet or even a planet, but it orbits a planet rather than a star.

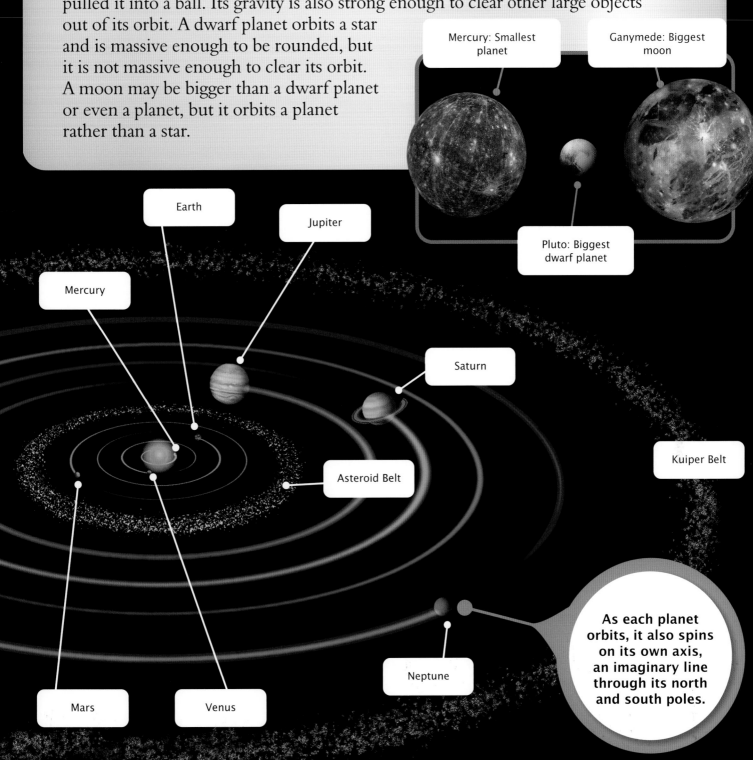

Mercury: Smallest planet

Ganymede: Biggest moon

Pluto: Biggest dwarf planet

Earth

Jupiter

Mercury

Saturn

Kuiper Belt

Asteroid Belt

As each planet orbits, it also spins on its own axis, an imaginary line through its north and south poles.

Neptune

Mars

Venus

The Big Bang

The Universe began 13.8 billion years ago in an event known as the Big Bang. In the first moment, the Universe started to expand from a very hot, very tiny point—and has been growing ever since.

Building Blocks

In the first moments after the Big Bang, there was no matter—nothing that could be seen or touched. Within the first second, tiny particles known as protons, neutrons, and electrons had been born. After 380,000 years, these particles had grouped together to form atoms. Atoms are the building blocks of all matter, from stars to planets to people. The earliest atoms were the lightest, simplest atoms: mostly hydrogen and helium.

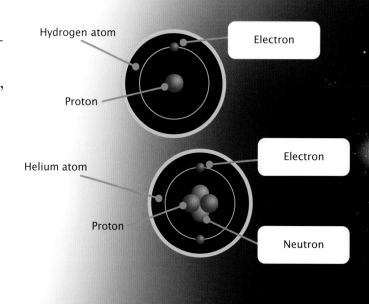

Hydrogen atom
Electron
Proton

Helium atom
Electron
Proton
Neutron

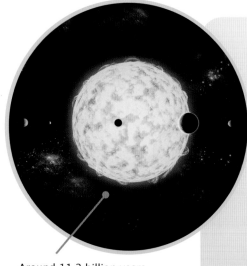

Around 11.2 billion years old, the star Kepler-444 is orbited by five planets.

Earliest Solar Systems

The earliest stars were not orbited by planets, because the heavy, complex atoms that make planets—such as iron and silicon—did not yet exist. In fact, these atoms formed inside the earliest stars and were blasted into space when the stars exploded in events known as supernovas. One of the earliest known solar systems in the Milky Way, called Kepler-444, formed about 2.6 billion years after the Big Bang.

DID YOU KNOW? Hydrogen and helium atoms make up 99.9 percent of all matter in the Universe.

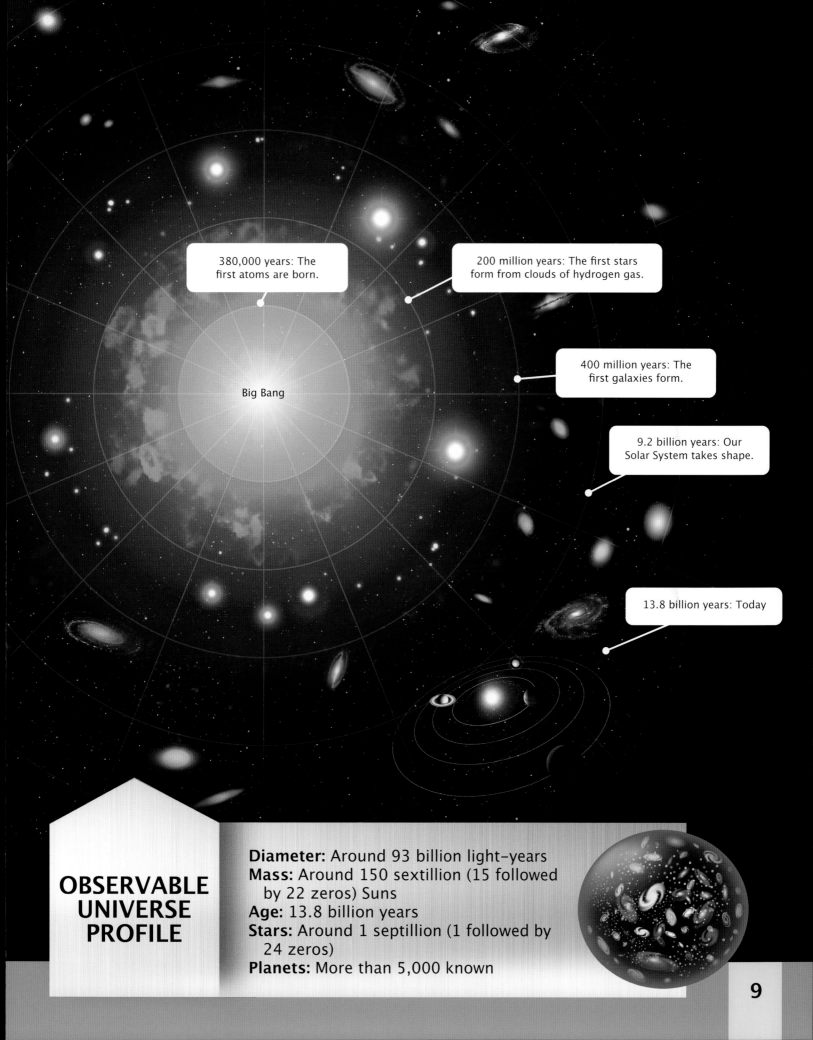

380,000 years: The first atoms are born.

200 million years: The first stars form from clouds of hydrogen gas.

400 million years: The first galaxies form.

9.2 billion years: Our Solar System takes shape.

13.8 billion years: Today

Big Bang

OBSERVABLE UNIVERSE PROFILE

Diameter: Around 93 billion light–years
Mass: Around 150 sextillion (15 followed by 22 zeros) Suns
Age: 13.8 billion years
Stars: Around 1 septillion (1 followed by 24 zeros)
Planets: More than 5,000 known

Birth of the Solar System

The Solar System is 4.6 billion years old. It started to form when a thick cloud of dust and gas was shaken by the explosion of a nearby star. The cloud collapsed, forming a clump that slowly became the Sun and its orbiting planets.

The Sun Forms

As the clump grew in the cloud of dust and hydrogen and helium gas, the clump's increasing mass increased the pull of its gravity. The clump pulled more material toward it, forming a spinning sphere of more and more tightly packed matter. Finally, the pressure in the core of the sphere was so great that hydrogen atoms started to smash together, combining to form helium atoms. This released an immense amount of energy, so the sphere began to give off light and heat—making it a star.

Jupiter formed around 1 million years after the Sun, about 100 million years before Earth.

The Sun probably formed in a cloud such as this one, which is about 2 light-years long and 8,500 light-years from Earth.

SOLAR SYSTEM PROFILE

Diameter: Around 26.9 billion km (16.7 billion miles)
Mass: 333,466 Earths
Age: 4.6 billion years
Planets: 8 known
Dwarf planets: 9 known
Moons: 219 known orbiting major planets

The Planets Form

A spinning disk of material, known as a protoplanetary disk, surrounded the brand-new star. Material in this disk began to clump together. Some clumps grew large enough for their own gravity to pull them into spheres, forming the planets, dwarf planets, and large moons.

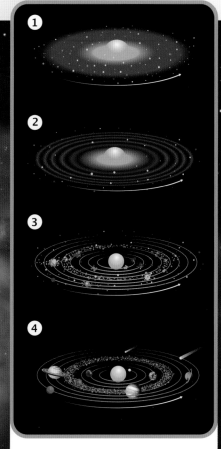

The Sun started to glow around 10 million years after the cloud collapse that set off the Solar System's formation.

The protoplanetary disk around the young Sun spun counterclockwise (anticlockwise), the same direction in which the planets orbit today.

KEY

1 The newly formed Sun is surrounded by a protoplanetary disk.
2 Gaps form in the disk as protoplanets (clumps that are developing into planets) start to sweep up the dust and gas around them.
3 The protoplanets continue to grow as they clear the areas around their orbits.
4 The planets are fully formed, while smaller, leftover pieces become asteroids, comets, and small moons.

DID YOU KNOW? Several other stars formed in the same cloud as the Sun, but these sister stars drifted apart and are scattered through the Milky Way.

11

Our Star

The Sun is a middle-sized, middle-aged star. In every second, 600 million tons of hydrogen are fused into helium in the Sun's core, a process that changes 4 million tons of matter into energy. This energy, which we see as light and feel as heat, is the key source of energy for life on Earth.

A Ball of Plasma

Like all stars, the Sun is a ball of super-hot plasma. Plasma is one of the four forms that matter can take: solid, liquid, gas, and plasma. A material can move through these states as it gets hotter. For example, water changes from a solid (ice) to liquid (water) to gas (water vapor) as its atoms gain energy and start moving faster and more freely. Plasma is rare on Earth but common in the Universe. In a plasma, the atoms are so hot that they break apart, losing some of their electrons (see page 8). This makes a plasma electrically charged.

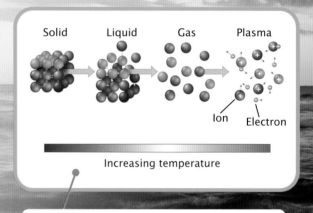

Increasing temperature

Electrons have a negative electric charge while protons have a positive electric charge. When atoms break apart in a plasma, the remaining portion of the atom, called an ion, has more protons than electrons, so it has a positive charge.

A Yellow Dwarf

The Sun is a type of star called a yellow dwarf. "Dwarf" tells us these stars are small compared to the largest stars, such as Betelgeuse, which is 764 times wider than the Sun. "Yellow" tells us that this type of star tends to shine with a yellow light because it is, for a star, medium hot. Hotter stars shine blue, while cooler stars shine red. However, brighter yellow dwarfs, including the Sun, actually shine white.

Despite being called a yellow dwarf, the Sun emits white light, as shown in this true image.

Around 73 percent of the Sun's mass is hydrogen, 25 percent is helium, and the rest includes oxygen, carbon, neon, and iron.

From Earth, we are used to seeing the Sun and surrounding sky look yellow, orange, or red due to Earth's atmosphere scattering the Sun's white light so it appears yellower (see pages 16–17).

Never look directly at the Sun as its brightness can cause serious eye damage or even blindness.

SUN PROFILE

Diameter: 1.39 million km (865,000 miles)
Mass: 332,950 Earths
Orbit around middle of Milky Way:
  Around 226 million years
Orbital speed: Around 864,000 km/h
  (536,865 miles per hour)
Rotation: Around 25 days
Rotation speed: Around 7,190 km/h (4,468 miles per hour)

DID YOU KNOW? The brightness of the Sun is equal to more than 4 septillion (4 followed by 24 zeros) household light bulbs.

The Sun's Structure

The Sun's core is where hydrogen is converted to helium, releasing energy in the form of tiny particles called photons. These packets of energy travel outward through the Sun's layers, before finally escaping into space from the star's surface, known as the photosphere.

Journey Through the Layers

From the core, photons must first travel through the Sun's radiation zone by a process called radiation: they bounce from atom to atom, losing a little energy with every bounce. It takes about 170,000 years for a photon to reach the Sun's next layer, the convection zone. Here, in the cooler, less-dense plasma, photons are carried by a process called convection: Like boiling water in a pan, hot bubbles of photon-carrying plasma rise to the photosphere. Finally, photons—which we see as light and feel as heat—stream into space.

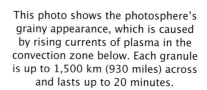

This photo shows the photosphere's grainy appearance, which is caused by rising currents of plasma in the convection zone below. Each granule is up to 1,500 km (930 miles) across and lasts up to 20 minutes.

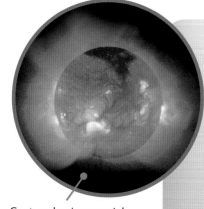

Captured using special instruments, this photo shows the Sun's corona extending far into space around the star.

Above the Surface

The Sun does not have a solid surface, but below the photosphere it is opaque (not see-through), making the photosphere the star's visible surface. Above the photosphere are layers of gas known as the chromosphere and corona. These layers of atmosphere are usually hidden by the brightness of the Sun's surface. Astronomers are not sure why, but the outer layer, the corona, is much hotter—at up to 1 million °C (1.8 million °F)—than the chromosphere, which is as cool as 3,500 °C (6,300 °F).

PHOTON PROFILE

Diameter: Infinitely small
Mass: 0
Speed in empty space: 299,792,458 m/s (983,571,056 ft per second)
Lifetime: At least 1 quintillion (1 followed by 18 zeros) years
Number emitted by the Sun: At least 1 quattuordecillion (1 followed by 45 zeros) per second

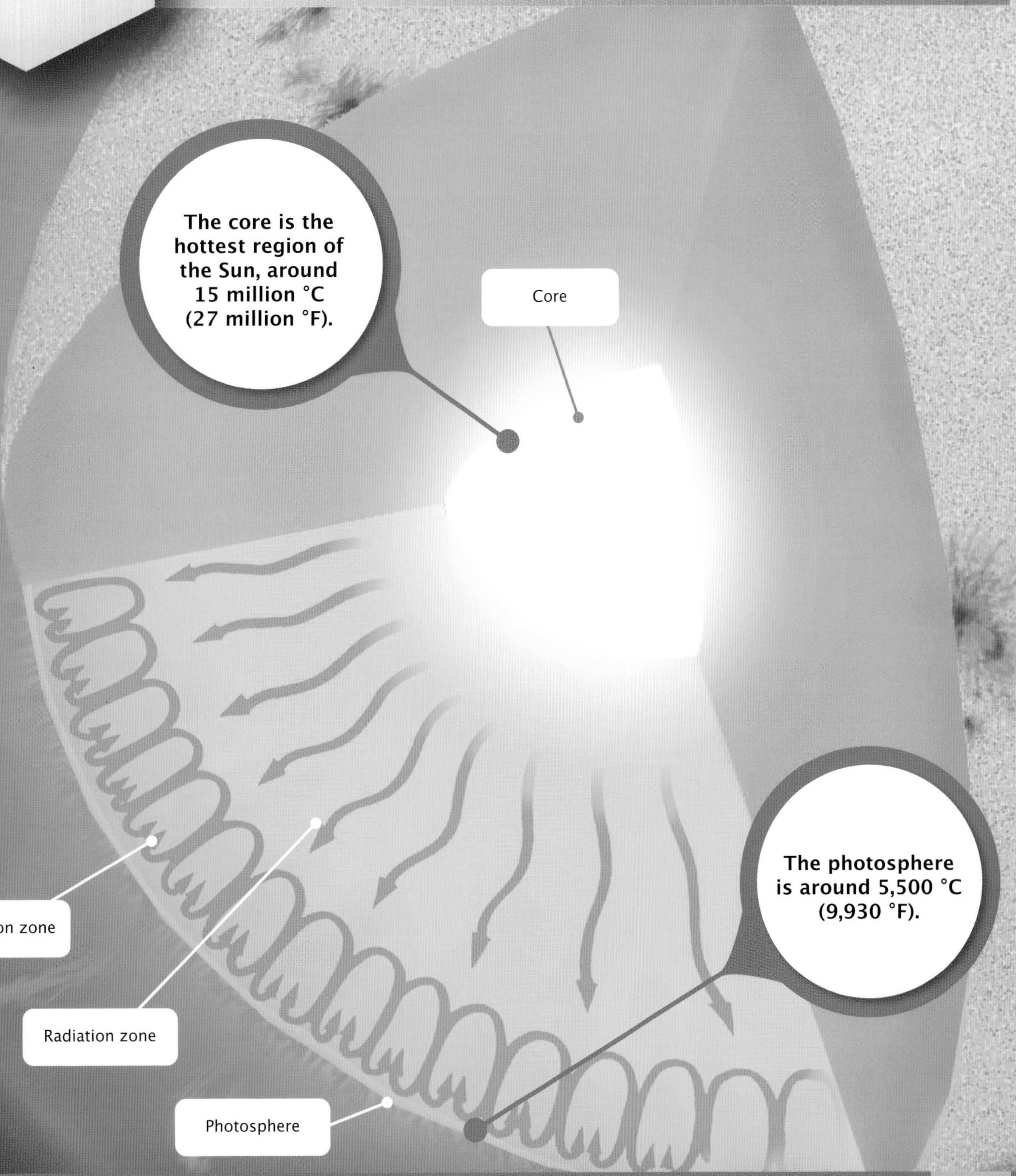

The core is the hottest region of the Sun, around 15 million °C (27 million °F).
Core
Convection zone
Radiation zone
Photosphere
The photosphere is around 5,500 °C (9,930 °F).

DID YOU KNOW? It takes 8 minutes for a photon to travel the 150 million km (93 million miles) from the Sun to Earth.

Solar Radiation

Solar radiation is the energy emitted by the Sun. The energy is emitted as photons, which travel in the form of waves. Different photons carry different amounts of energy and have different wavelengths: the distances between the crest of one wave and the next. Some wavelengths are visible to humans as light, but others are invisible.

The Electromagnetic Spectrum

The range of energy released by the Sun is known as the electromagnetic spectrum. At one end of the spectrum are low-energy photons, which have long wavelengths. At the opposite end are high-energy photons, which have short wavelengths.

Sunlight usually looks white, but it is a mixture of all the shades of the rainbow.

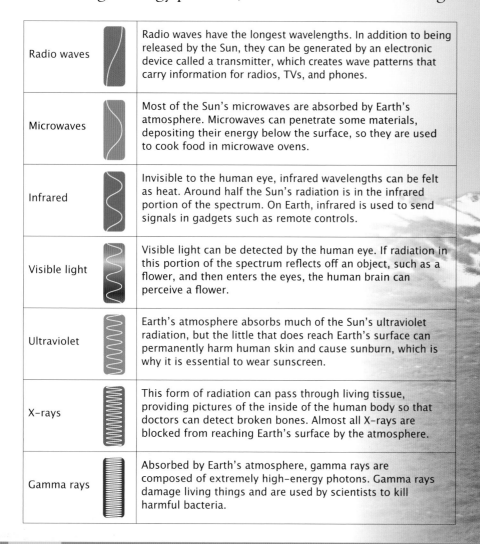

Radio waves	Radio waves have the longest wavelengths. In addition to being released by the Sun, they can be generated by an electronic device called a transmitter, which creates wave patterns that carry information for radios, TVs, and phones.
Microwaves	Most of the Sun's microwaves are absorbed by Earth's atmosphere. Microwaves can penetrate some materials, depositing their energy below the surface, so they are used to cook food in microwave ovens.
Infrared	Invisible to the human eye, infrared wavelengths can be felt as heat. Around half the Sun's radiation is in the infrared portion of the spectrum. On Earth, infrared is used to send signals in gadgets such as remote controls.
Visible light	Visible light can be detected by the human eye. If radiation in this portion of the spectrum reflects off an object, such as a flower, and then enters the eyes, the human brain can perceive a flower.
Ultraviolet	Earth's atmosphere absorbs much of the Sun's ultraviolet radiation, but the little that does reach Earth's surface can permanently harm human skin and cause sunburn, which is why it is essential to wear sunscreen.
X-rays	This form of radiation can pass through living tissue, providing pictures of the inside of the human body so that doctors can detect broken bones. Almost all X-rays are blocked from reaching Earth's surface by the atmosphere.
Gamma rays	Absorbed by Earth's atmosphere, gamma rays are composed of extremely high-energy photons. Gamma rays damage living things and are used by scientists to kill harmful bacteria.

When sunlight passes through raindrops, each wavelength of visible light is bent at a different angle, resulting in its separation into a rainbow.

DID YOU KNOW? Most solar radiation is in the infrared, visible light, and ultraviolet parts of the electromagnetic spectrum.

Visible Light

The main source of visible light on Earth is the Sun, but it is also emitted by electric lights and flames. Visible light looks white, but it is made up of all the shades of the rainbow. Each shade has a different wavelength. Visible light can pass through some materials, such as glass and water, but not others. When light hits an opaque object, some wavelengths are absorbed and some are reflected. When we see an object of a particular shade, that wavelength of light is being reflected and the others are being absorbed.

A green object absorbs all wavelengths except green, which it reflects into human eyes.

A black object absorbs all wavelengths, so human eyes see it as black.

A white object reflects all wavelengths into human eyes, which see it as white.

SOLAR RADIATION WAVELENGTHS

Radio waves: 100,000 km to 1 m (62,000 miles to 3.3 ft)
Microwaves: 1 m to 1 mm (3.3 ft to 0.039 in)
Infrared: 1 to 0.00075 mm (0.039 to 0.00003 in)
Visible light: 0.00075 to 0.00038 mm (0.00003 to 0.000015 in)
Ultraviolet: 0.00038 to 0.000001 mm (0.000015 to 0.00000004 in)
X-rays: 0.000001 to 0.000000001 mm (0.00000004 to 0.00000000004 in)
Gamma rays: Less than 0.000000001 mm (0.00000000004 in)

The Solar Cycle

The Sun's appearance is not uniform or unchanging: With the help of special equipment, features such as sunspots, flares, and loops can be observed. These features are caused by the Sun's magnetic activity, which changes over an 11-year period known as the solar cycle.

This photograph of the Sun was taken by the Solar Dynamics Observatory, an Earth–orbiting satellite.

The Sun's Magnetic Fields

Magnetism is a force caused by the movement of electric charges. Since the Sun's plasma is electrically charged (see page 12), its movement creates powerful magnetism known as magnetic fields. As plasma rises and falls, the Sun's magnetic fields twist and tangle, creating eruptions of plasma and energy at the surface. Over an 11-year period, this activity peaks then dies away, as the magnetic fields smooth out again.

Magnetic fields attract or repel magnets, as well as affecting the movement of electrically charged particles, such as those in plasma.

SOLAR CYCLE 25

The 25th cycle since 1755, when monitoring began

Cycle began (last solar minimum): December 2019
Cycle ends (next solar minimum): Around 2030
Solar maximum: Around 2025
**Estimated number of sunspots
   at solar maximum:** Around 150 at one time

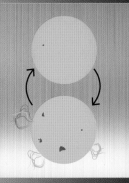

DID YOU KNOW? In 1859, an intense coronal mass ejection started electrical fires on Earth and caused intensely bright lights in Earth's atmosphere, known as auroras.

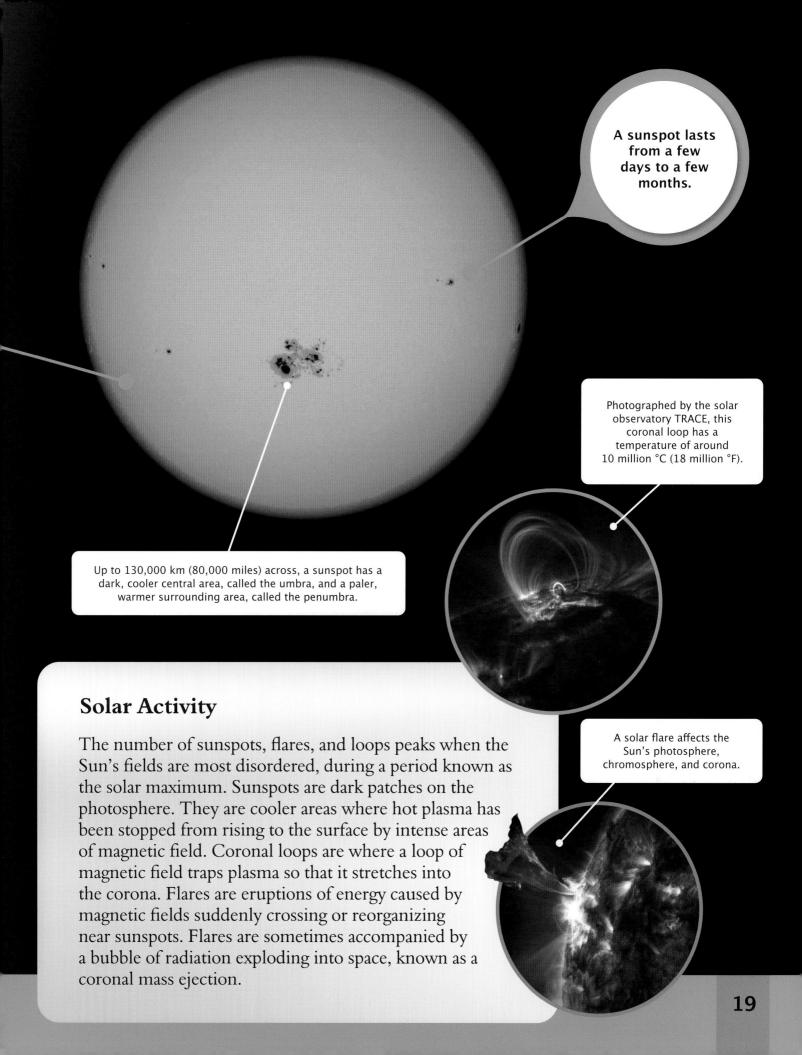

A sunspot lasts from a few days to a few months.

Photographed by the solar observatory TRACE, this coronal loop has a temperature of around 10 million °C (18 million °F).

Up to 130,000 km (80,000 miles) across, a sunspot has a dark, cooler central area, called the umbra, and a paler, warmer surrounding area, called the penumbra.

A solar flare affects the Sun's photosphere, chromosphere, and corona.

Solar Activity

The number of sunspots, flares, and loops peaks when the Sun's fields are most disordered, during a period known as the solar maximum. Sunspots are dark patches on the photosphere. They are cooler areas where hot plasma has been stopped from rising to the surface by intense areas of magnetic field. Coronal loops are where a loop of magnetic field traps plasma so that it stretches into the corona. Flares are eruptions of energy caused by magnetic fields suddenly crossing or reorganizing near sunspots. Flares are sometimes accompanied by a bubble of radiation exploding into space, known as a coronal mass ejection.

Solar Eclipses

A solar eclipse is when, as the Moon passes between Earth and the Sun, it partly or totally blocks the view of our star from a region of Earth's surface. Special eye protection or viewing equipment is essential when watching an eclipse to prevent permanent eye damage.

During a total solar eclipse, the sky darkens, the temperature falls, and birds may stop singing because they believe it is night-time.

Partial or Total

As the Moon orbits Earth, it passes between the Sun and Earth once every 27.3 days. Yet a total eclipse can be seen somewhere on Earth only every 18 months on average. This is because the Moon's orbit around Earth is tilted around 5 degrees away from Earth's orbit around the Sun, so the Moon does not frequently line up exactly with the Sun and Earth. In addition, the Moon's orbit is not exactly circular so—even when the Moon does line up—it may be too far from Earth to block the Sun's face entirely.

An annular solar eclipse is when the Moon lines up between the Sun and Earth but is too far away to cover the Sun's disk completely. Annular eclipses are about as common as total eclipses.

A partial solar eclipse is when the Moon partly covers the Sun's disk. Partial eclipses are a little more common than total eclipses.

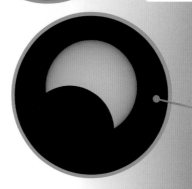

This photograph was taken the last time Venus transited the Sun, in 2012.

Transits

A transit of the Sun is when one of the planets that is closer to the star than Earth—Mercury and Venus—appears to cross its disk. The more distant planets cannot pass between Earth and the Sun. Mercury transits 13 or 14 times every century, always in May or November. The next Mercury transit will be in November 2032. Venus transits much more rarely, with the next taking place in 2117.

When the Sun's photosphere is completely covered, the glowing corona can be seen.

A total solar eclipse is visible from a narrow band across Earth's surface that falls in the path of the Moon's full shadow.

SOLAR ECLIPSES OF 21st CENTURY

Number: 224 (77 partial, 73 annular, 68 total, and 6 a combination of total and annular)
Most eclipses in a year: 4 (in 2011, 2029, 2047, 2065, 2076, and 2094)
Longest possible duration of a total eclipse at any location: 7 minutes 32 seconds
Only year with 2 total eclipses: 2057

Total eclipse

Partial eclipse

DID YOU KNOW? A particular town or city on Earth's surface is likely to experience a total solar eclipse only once every 360 to 410 years.

The Heliosphere

The heliosphere is a bubble-like region of space that surrounds the Sun, stretching far beyond the outermost orbiting planet. The heliosphere is filled by the solar wind, a stream of electrically charged particles that flows constantly from the Sun's corona.

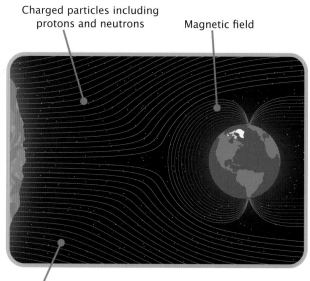

Charged particles including protons and neutrons

Magnetic field

Earth's magnetic field makes most of the solar wind's high-energy particles flow around and beyond our planet.

The Solar Wind

The solar wind blows a bubble—also containing dust and hydrogen—in the interstellar medium, which is the matter that fills the space between the solar systems of a galaxy. The interstellar medium is composed of gas (mostly hydrogen and helium), dust, and high-energy particles. Earth is protected from the solar wind by its magnetic field (see pages 36–37).

Regions of the Heliosphere

The inner region of the heliosphere is where the solar wind blows fastest. This region ends at the termination shock. Beyond the termination shock is the heliosheath, an outer, stormy region of the heliosphere where the solar wind is buffeted by winds from outer space. The outer edge of the heliosphere is known as the heliopause. This is where the solar wind is no longer strong enough to push back the interstellar medium. Many astronomers define the heliopause as the edge of the Solar System.

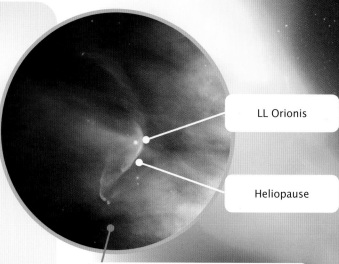

LL Orionis

Heliopause

The Hubble Space Telescope took this photograph of the heliosphere of the star LL Orionis, which is believed to have a similar structure to the Sun's.

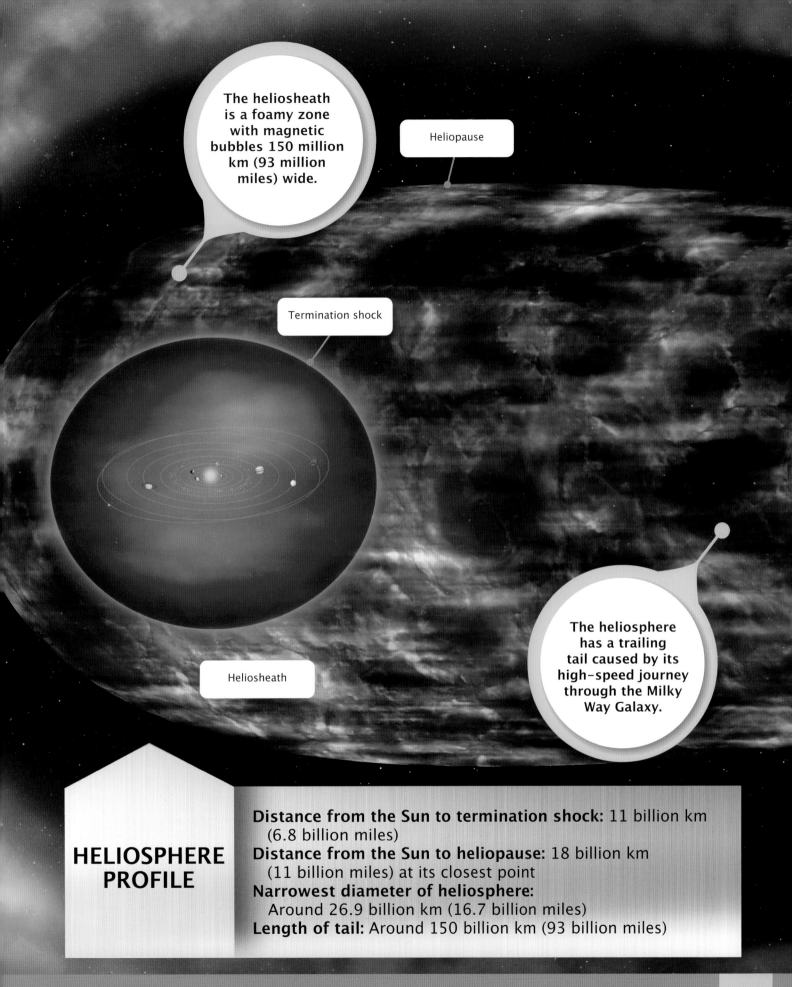

The heliosheath is a foamy zone with magnetic bubbles 150 million km (93 million miles) wide.

Heliopause

Termination shock

Heliosheath

The heliosphere has a trailing tail caused by its high-speed journey through the Milky Way Galaxy.

HELIOSPHERE PROFILE

Distance from the Sun to termination shock: 11 billion km (6.8 billion miles)

Distance from the Sun to heliopause: 18 billion km (11 billion miles) at its closest point

Narrowest diameter of heliosphere: Around 26.9 billion km (16.7 billion miles)

Length of tail: Around 150 billion km (93 billion miles)

DID YOU KNOW? In the region of Earth, the solar wind travels at between 250 and 750 km/s (155 and 465 miles per second).

Death of the Sun

In around 6 billion years, the Sun will throw out a cloud of hot gas known as a planetary nebula.

Like all stars, the Sun was born and will die. In around 5 billion years, the Sun will run out of the fuel that makes it glow: hydrogen. The Sun will start to die, destroying Earth and the other Solar System planets.

A Slow Death

After the Sun runs out of hydrogen, its outer layers will expand, turning the Sun into a red giant star around 110 million km (70 million miles) across. This will destroy Mercury and Venus—and bake Earth. For around 1 billion years, the red giant Sun will use its helium as fuel. When that runs out, the Sun will shed its outer layers, making a glowing cloud of gas and dust known as a planetary nebula. A dense core of material, known as a white dwarf, will be left behind. Over trillions of years, the white dwarf will probably cool and fade into a black dwarf.

The Sun will eventually fade into a black dwarf, which will emit no heat or light. It takes so long to become a black dwarf that there are none yet in existence in the Universe.

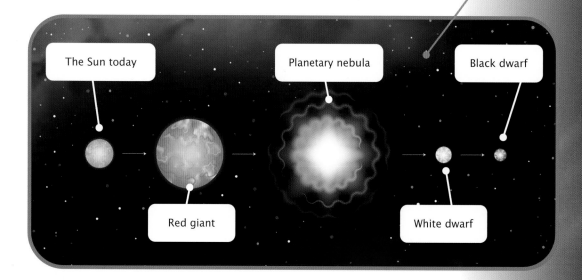

The Sun today

Red giant

Planetary nebula

White dwarf

Black dwarf

DID YOU KNOW? The most massive stars use up their fuel within a few hundreds of millions of years, but the smallest stars could survive hundreds of billions of years.

Although it will no longer be producing energy from its fuel, the dying Sun will still be around 100,000 °C (180,000 °F).

The Solar System's remaining planets will be destroyed, with Neptune boiling away perhaps a few hundred million years after Earth has been obliterated.

A black hole is a region where so much mass is squeezed into so little space that its gravity deforms space. If anything comes too near a black hole, it is pulled inside.

Different Deaths

If stars are between 0.3 and 8 times the Sun's mass, they die in the same manner as our star. Smaller stars shrink straight into white dwarfs when they use up their hydrogen. When a larger star runs out of fuel, its core collapses, throwing out energy in an explosion known as a supernova. A supernova leaves behind a tiny, very dense neutron star or—in the case of stars more than 20 times the mass of the Sun—a black hole.

Chapter 2

Earth and the Moon

This photo of Earth and the Moon was taken from the *Apollo 11* spacecraft in July 1969, shortly before its astronauts became the first humans to land on the Moon.

The planet we call home is the third planet from the Sun. Earth formed around 4.54 billion years ago in the gas and dust spinning around the young Sun. Earth's companion, the Moon, has been orbiting our planet for around the past 4.51 billion years.

Formation of Earth and the Moon

Earth formed when gas and dust clumped together. As the clump grew, its gravity pulled in more material, making a ball of mixed rock and metal. The ball was so hot the metal melted and—being denser than the rock—sank to the new planet's core. Within the next few million years, astronomers think Earth was hit by a smaller planet. The impact threw out rubble that, pulled both by Earth's gravity and its own, formed a sphere: the Moon. After this impact, the molten Earth released gases, creating an atmosphere.

Earth is a molten ball of rock and metal.

Earth is hit by a smaller planet, which astronomers call Theia.

The impact melts Earth and throws out rubble.

The rubble is pulled into a sphere, the Moon.

An atmosphere forms around Earth.

As Earth cools, clouds form in the atmosphere, and—by around 4.4 billion years ago—rain fills the oceans.

DID YOU KNOW? At 27 percent of Earth's size, the Moon is larger compared to its host planet than any other moon in the Solar System.

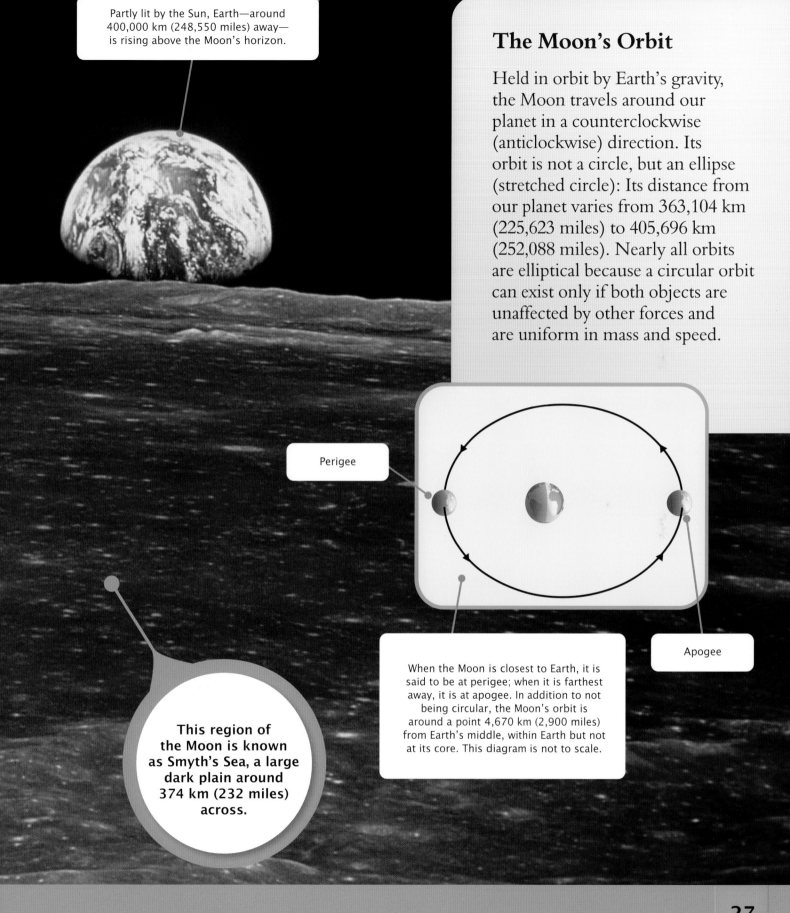

Partly lit by the Sun, Earth—around 400,000 km (248,550 miles) away—is rising above the Moon's horizon.

The Moon's Orbit

Held in orbit by Earth's gravity, the Moon travels around our planet in a counterclockwise (anticlockwise) direction. Its orbit is not a circle, but an ellipse (stretched circle): Its distance from our planet varies from 363,104 km (225,623 miles) to 405,696 km (252,088 miles). Nearly all orbits are elliptical because a circular orbit can exist only if both objects are unaffected by other forces and are uniform in mass and speed.

Perigee

Apogee

When the Moon is closest to Earth, it is said to be at perigee; when it is farthest away, it is at apogee. In addition to not being circular, the Moon's orbit is around a point 4,670 km (2,900 miles) from Earth's middle, within Earth but not at its core. This diagram is not to scale.

This region of the Moon is known as Smyth's Sea, a large dark plain around 374 km (232 miles) across.

Earth's Structure

Earth has four layers: its inner core, outer core, mantle, and crust. The crust, made of rock, is cool enough for animals and plants to live on. The inner core, made of metal, is around 5,400 °C (9,700 °F), which is about as hot as the surface of the Sun.

Earth's Layers

Earth's inner and outer core are made mostly of super-hot iron and nickel. Much of the core's heat is left over from the planet's violent formation. In the outer core, the metal is so hot it is liquid. In the inner core, the metal is squeezed so tightly it is solid. The mantle is made of rock as hot as 3,700 °C (6,690 °F). In places, the rock in the mantle melts, when it is known as magma. The mantle flows very slowly as currents of hot rock rise. Earth's solid rock crust has an average surface temperature of 14 °C (57 °F).

Under the oceans, Earth's crust—known as the oceanic crust—is only 5 to 10 km (3 to 6 miles) thick.

Inner core: Depth of 5,150 to 6,378 km (3,200 to 3,963 miles)

Outer core: Depth of 2,890 to 5,150 km (1,795 to 3,200 miles)

Mantle: Depth of 70 to 2,890 km (45 to 1,795 miles)

Crust: Depth of 0 to 70 km (0 to 45 miles)

EARTH PROFILE

Diameter: 12,756 km (7,926 miles)
Mass: 0.000003 Suns
Average distance from the Sun:
  149.6 million km (92.9 million miles)
Orbit: 365.25 days
Rotation: 23.93 hours
Moons: 1

DID YOU KNOW? The distance around Earth's equator (an imaginary line dividing it into northern and southern halves) is 40,075 km (24,901 miles).

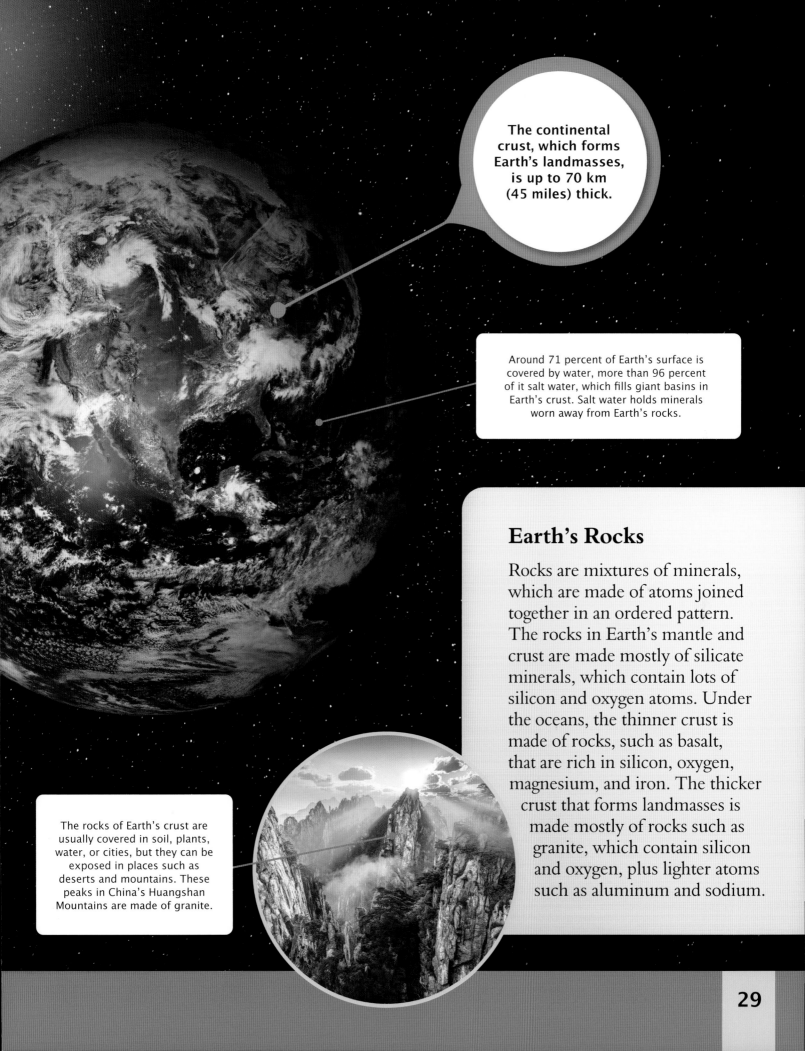

The continental crust, which forms Earth's landmasses, is up to 70 km (45 miles) thick.

Around 71 percent of Earth's surface is covered by water, more than 96 percent of it salt water, which fills giant basins in Earth's crust. Salt water holds minerals worn away from Earth's rocks.

Earth's Rocks

Rocks are mixtures of minerals, which are made of atoms joined together in an ordered pattern. The rocks in Earth's mantle and crust are made mostly of silicate minerals, which contain lots of silicon and oxygen atoms. Under the oceans, the thinner crust is made of rocks, such as basalt, that are rich in silicon, oxygen, magnesium, and iron. The thicker crust that forms landmasses is made mostly of rocks such as granite, which contain silicon and oxygen, plus lighter atoms such as aluminum and sodium.

The rocks of Earth's crust are usually covered in soil, plants, water, or cities, but they can be exposed in places such as deserts and mountains. These peaks in China's Huangshan Mountains are made of granite.

Changing Planet

Earth's crust, along with the top portion of the mantle, is broken into giant plates of rock, known as tectonic plates. These plates float on the slowly moving mantle below, causing changes to our planet's surface both very slowly—and very fast.

Changing Continents

Around 3 to 4 billion years ago, as Earth cooled, the crust and upper mantle cracked into seven large, major plates and many smaller, minor plates. On average, the plates move by 3 to 5 cm (1.2 to 2 in) a year. Yet, over millions and billions of years, plate movement has rearranged the continents, created new oceans, and—where plates are moving toward each other—pushed up mountain ranges as the rock crumpled and folded.

The volcano Tungurahua, in Ecuador, formed where the minor Nazca Plate is moving under the South American Plate.

225 million years ago

Pangaea

150 million years ago

66 million years ago

North America Europe Asia

Africa India

South America

Australia

Antarctica

Around 225 million years ago, the continents were joined as one supercontinent called Pangaea. By 66 million years ago, when the dinosaurs became extinct, the continents were beginning to take the shape they have today.

MAJOR TECTONIC PLATES

Pacific: 103.3 million sq km (39.9 million sq miles)
North American: 75.9 million sq km (29.3 million sq miles)
Eurasian: 67.8 million sq km (26.2 million sq miles)
African: 61.3 million sq km (23.7 million sq miles)
Antarctic: 60.9 million sq km (23.5 million sq miles)
Australian: 47 million sq km (18 million sq miles)
South American: 43.6 million sq km (16.8 million sq miles)

Volcanoes and Earthquakes

Most volcanoes and earthquakes happen near the edges of tectonic plates. A volcano is a hole in the crust through which magma surges to the surface. An earthquake happens when two plates get stuck on each other as they move—then suddenly break free, shaking the ground.

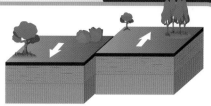

Where plates are moving past each other, known as a transform boundary, earthquakes can happen.

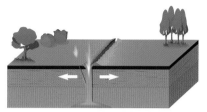

Where plates are moving apart, known as a divergent boundary, earthquakes can happen and magma wells up, forming volcanoes.

Where plates are moving toward each other, known as a convergent boundary, large earthquakes can happen and magma is forced to the surface, often forming lines of volcanoes.

When magma reaches Earth's surface, it is known as lava.

A volcano can grow into a mountain as lava from eruption after eruption cools and hardens into solid rock.

DID YOU KNOW? Earth's tallest mountain, Mt Everest, currently 8,849 m (29,032 ft), grows by 4 mm (0.16 in) a year due to the collision of the Indian and Eurasian Plates.

31

Earth's Orbit

Earth's elliptical, counterclockwise orbit round the Sun takes about 365.25 days. Every four years, we add an extra day to the calendar, February 29, so the calendar year—usually 365 days— keeps pace with Earth's orbit. Earth also rotates counterclockwise around its own axis, an imaginary line through its North and South Poles.

Seasons

Earth's axis is not at right angles to the plane of its orbit: It is tilted by 23.4 degrees. It is this axial tilt that causes seasons on Earth. When the northern hemisphere is tilted toward the Sun, it has summer, with hotter weather. At the same time, the southern hemisphere has winter.

In Sweden, in northern Europe, people celebrate the longest day of the year, known as the summer solstice, with traditional music.

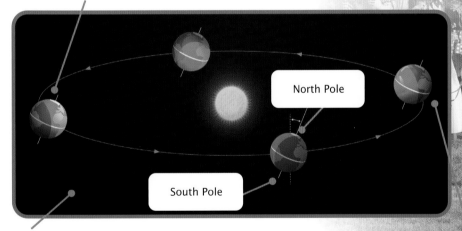

Summer in the northern hemisphere

North Pole

South Pole

Astronomers think it may have been the collision with Theia (see page 26) that knocked Earth to one side, resulting in seasons.

Summer in the southern hemisphere

EARTH'S ORBIT

Distance of one orbit: 942 million km (585 million miles)
Average orbital speed: 107,200 km/h (66,600 miles per hour)
Perihelion (shortest distance to the Sun): Around January 3
Perihelion distance: 147 million km (91.4 million miles)
Aphelion (farthest distance to the Sun): Around July 4
Aphelion distance: 152.1 million km (94.5 million miles)

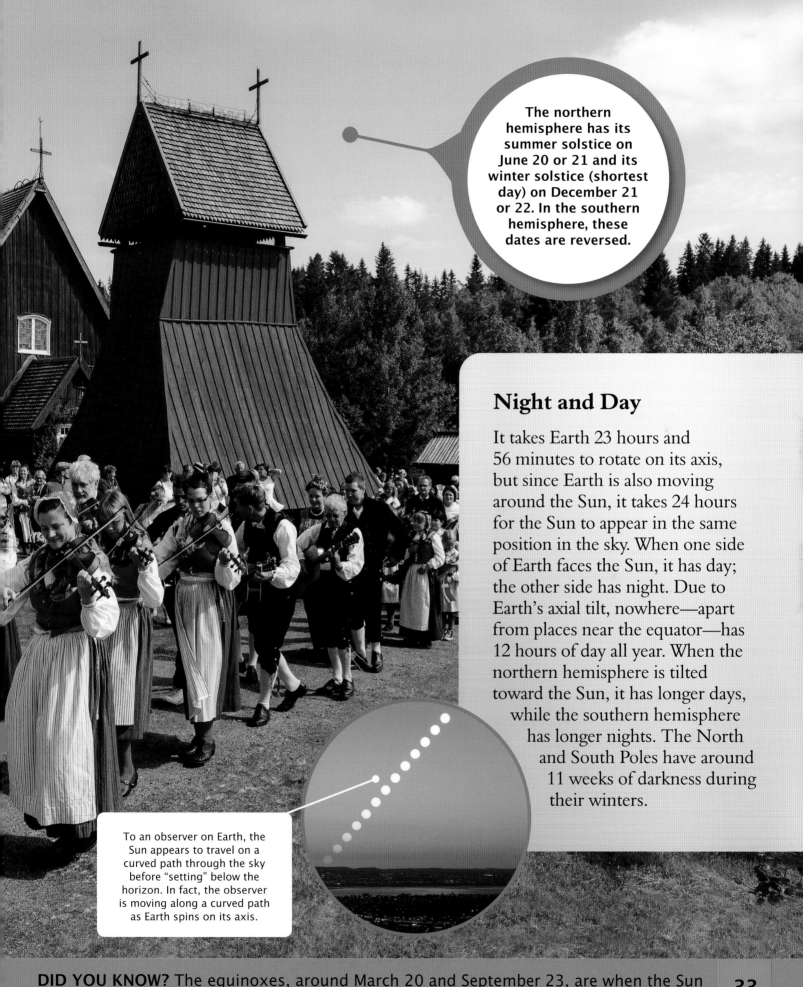

The northern hemisphere has its summer solstice on June 20 or 21 and its winter solstice (shortest day) on December 21 or 22. In the southern hemisphere, these dates are reversed.

Night and Day

It takes Earth 23 hours and 56 minutes to rotate on its axis, but since Earth is also moving around the Sun, it takes 24 hours for the Sun to appear in the same position in the sky. When one side of Earth faces the Sun, it has day; the other side has night. Due to Earth's axial tilt, nowhere—apart from places near the equator—has 12 hours of day all year. When the northern hemisphere is tilted toward the Sun, it has longer days, while the southern hemisphere has longer nights. The North and South Poles have around 11 weeks of darkness during their winters.

To an observer on Earth, the Sun appears to travel on a curved path through the sky before "setting" below the horizon. In fact, the observer is moving along a curved path as Earth spins on its axis.

DID YOU KNOW? The equinoxes, around March 20 and September 23, are when the Sun is directly overhead at the equator and everywhere has around 12 hours of daylight.

33

The Atmosphere

Earth is the only place in the Universe where life is known to exist. Life as we know it would not exist without the atmosphere, a mixture of gases held around Earth by its gravity. The atmosphere supplies us with water and the gas oxygen, while also trapping enough of the Sun's heat to help keep Earth the right temperature for life.

The atmosphere presses down on Earth, keeping liquid surface water from drifting into space.

Essential Air

The atmosphere, also known as "air," is around 21 percent oxygen. Animals need to breathe oxygen to supply their body's cells with energy. Scientists divide the atmosphere into layers, each less tightly packed with air than the one below, as the pull of Earth's gravity weakens.

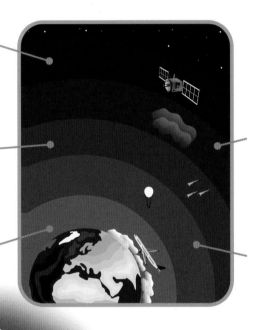

Exosphere: To 10,000 km (6,200 miles)
Many human-made satellites circle Earth in the exosphere.

Mesosphere: To 80 km (50 miles)
This is where most space rocks burn up, creating meteor showers (see page 100).

Troposphere: To 12 km (7 miles)
Passenger planes fly in this layer, where most clouds form.

Thermosphere: To 600 km (370 miles)
The thermosphere is where auroras can be seen (see page 36).

Stratosphere: To 50 km (30 miles)
Weather balloons float into this layer so scientists can monitor the atmosphere.

GASES IN EARTH'S ATMOSPHERE

Nitrogen: Around 77.7 percent
Oxygen: Around 20.9 percent
Argon: Around 0.9 percent
Water vapor: Around 0.4 percent
Carbon dioxide, neon, helium, methane, krypton, and others: Around 0.1 percent

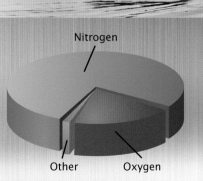

Nitrogen

Other

Oxygen

The Water Cycle

The water cycle is the movement of water from Earth to the atmosphere and back again. As the Sun heats oceans, rivers, and lakes, some water evaporates, turning into an invisible gas known as water vapor. The water vapor floats into the atmosphere, where it cools. This makes some of the water vapor condense into drops of liquid water, which we see as clouds. When the drops become too big to float, they fall to the ground, which is known as precipitation. The water cycle gives animals and plants the water they need to transport materials through their body.

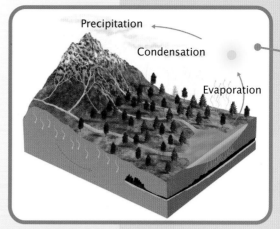

Precipitation

Condensation

Evaporation

Scientists think Earth's water cycle began around 4.4 billion years ago, when rain filled the early oceans. It was in the oceans that the first, simple life forms appeared around 4 billion years ago.

All life on Earth—from bacteria to trees to elephants—needs water to survive. Nearly all Earth's living things also need oxygen, which is found in air and water.

Earth is an ideal distance from the Sun for liquid water: If Earth were perhaps 7 million km (4.3 million miles) closer, its water would boil into steam, yet if Earth were perhaps 100 million km (62 million miles) farther away, all its water would freeze.

DID YOU KNOW? The daytime sky looks blue because the atmosphere scatters the Sun's waves of blue light more than its other waves, making blue light more visible.

Auroras

Lights, known as auroras, can be seen in the night sky around Earth's poles. They are caused by gases in the atmosphere being given energy by particles from the Sun. The particles are deflected toward Earth's poles by our planet's magnetic field.

A patchy, pulsating aurora is caused by high-energy particles being scattered into the atmosphere.

Earth's Magnetic Field

Magnetism is a force that can be made by the movement of electric current through magnetic metals, such as iron. All materials are made of atoms, which have tiny particles called electrons spinning around their core (see page 8). Electric current is a flow of electrons from atom to atom. As molten iron churns in Earth's outer core, its electrons flow, generating a magnetic field that extends far into space.

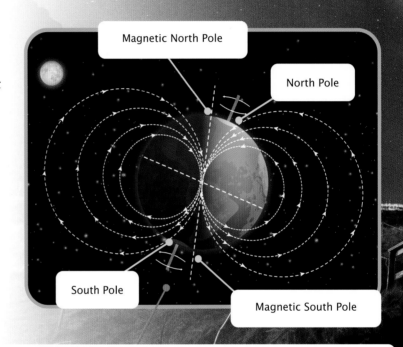

Magnetic North Pole

North Pole

South Pole

Magnetic South Pole

Earth is a giant magnet with—like all magnets—a north pole and a south pole. Magnetic force flows from one pole to the other, due to the coordinated movements of the electrons in Earth's outer core. Earth's magnetic poles are around 500 km (310 miles) from the north and south poles of its axis of rotation.

AURORAS

Green light: Given off by oxygen at heights of 100 to 300 km (60 to 185 miles)

Orange-red light: Given off by very excited oxygen at heights of 300 to 400 km (185 to 250 miles)

Pink, purple, and dark red light: Given off by nitrogen at heights of 80 to 100 km (50 to 60 miles)

Blue and purple light: Given off by hydrogen and helium but usually difficult to see against the night sky

DID YOU KNOW? Mercury is the only Solar System planet that does not experience auroras, as it does not have enough of an atmosphere to be excited by the solar wind.

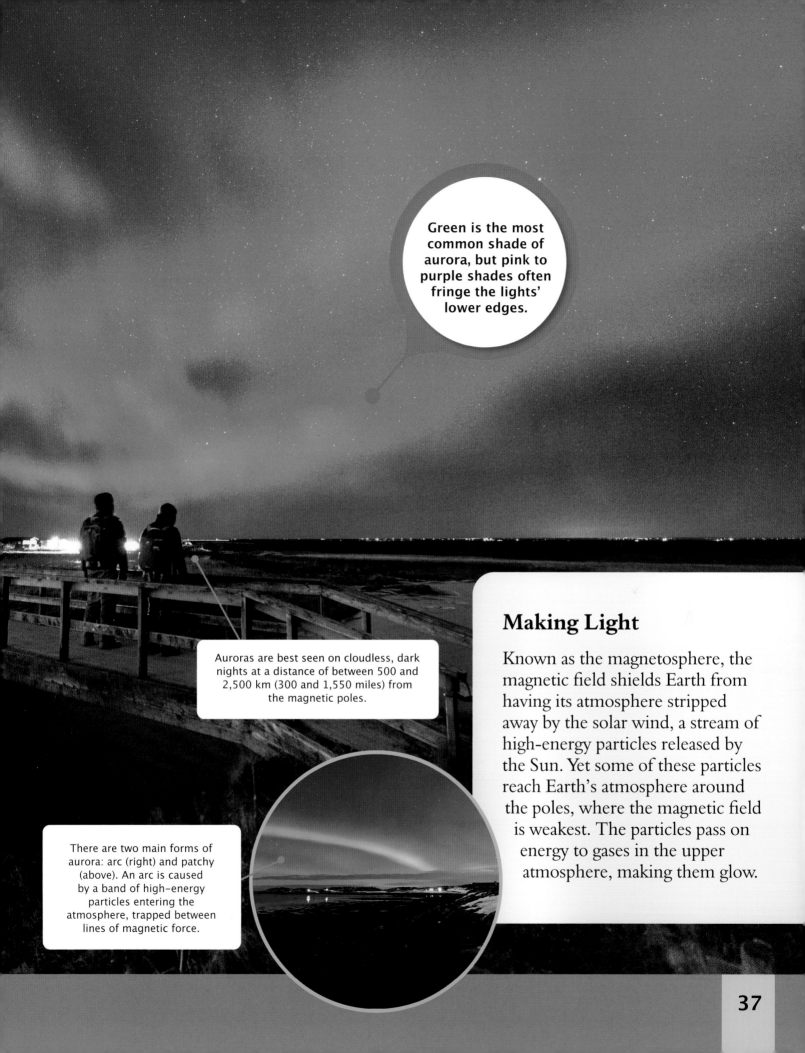

Green is the most common shade of aurora, but pink to purple shades often fringe the lights' lower edges.

Auroras are best seen on cloudless, dark nights at a distance of between 500 and 2,500 km (300 and 1,550 miles) from the magnetic poles.

There are two main forms of aurora: arc (right) and patchy (above). An arc is caused by a band of high-energy particles entering the atmosphere, trapped between lines of magnetic force.

Making Light

Known as the magnetosphere, the magnetic field shields Earth from having its atmosphere stripped away by the solar wind, a stream of high-energy particles released by the Sun. Yet some of these particles reach Earth's atmosphere around the poles, where the magnetic field is weakest. The particles pass on energy to gases in the upper atmosphere, making them glow.

The Moon

The Moon is a ball of rock and metal. Like Earth and the other planets, the Moon is not a perfect sphere but an oblate spheroid: a ball that bulges slightly at its equator due to its rotation—a little like a ball of dough flattening into a pizza as it is spun by a chef.

The Moon's Structure

For the Moon's first 100 million years it was molten. As it cooled, metal—mostly iron—sank to the core, while the least dense rocks floated to the surface. Like Earth, the Moon has an inner core of solid metal and an outer core of liquid metal. Since the Moon is much smaller than Earth, it cooled faster: The temperature of its inner core is only around 1,300 °C (2,370 °F). Around the core is a mantle of partly melted rock. The Moon's outer layer is a crust of solid rock.

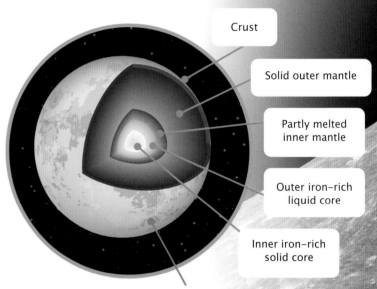

Crust

Solid outer mantle

Partly melted inner mantle

Outer iron-rich liquid core

Inner iron-rich solid core

The Moon's outer core of liquid iron is too small and cool to generate more than a weak magnetic field.

The far side of the Moon, seen here in a photo taken by the space probe *Lunar Reconnaissance Orbiter*, has a thicker crust and fewer dark "seas" (see page 40) than the near side.

Only One Side

From Earth, we can only see one side of the Moon, often called the "near side." This is because the Moon rotates in exactly the same time as it travels around Earth, resulting in it keeping nearly the same face turned toward our planet. This phenomenon is known as tidal locking. All the large moons in the Solar System are tidally locked with their planet. Moons that orbit close to their planet usually become tidally locked within 100 million years of their formation, as their rotation slows to match their orbit due to the pull of the planet's gravity.

DID YOU KNOW? Since the Moon's mass is smaller than Earth's, its surface gravity is one-sixth of Earth's—so astronauts can jump much higher on the Moon.

The Moon has an extremely thin atmosphere containing gases such as helium and argon.

The crust—made of rocks including basalt and anorthosite, which are common on Earth—is covered by dusty fragments of rock known as regolith.

Without a thick atmosphere to both shield from the Sun's rays and hold on to their warmth, the Moon's surface has extremes of temperature: up to 120 °C (250 °F) at the equator during the day and down to –253 °C (–424 °F) at the poles during the night.

THE MOON PROFILE

Diameter: 3,475 km (2,159 miles)
Mass: 0.012 Earths
Average distance from Earth: 384,400 km (238,855 miles)
Orbit around Earth: 27.3 days
Rotation: 27.3 days

Craters and Seas

The Moon is marked by thousands of craters, made when asteroids and comets crashed into its surface. The dark patches we can see on the Moon are areas of ancient hardened lava. These were once thought to be filled with water, which is why they are known as "seas."

Impact Craters

The near side of the Moon has around 300,000 craters wider than 1 km (0.6 miles), while the far side is even more heavily cratered. Since the Moon has little atmosphere—which would burn up smaller space rocks before impact—it has been more heavily impacted than Earth. With no water or wind on the Moon to wear away its surface, its craters remain much as they were when they were made, even if that was billions of years ago.

Like most of the Moon's craters, Moltke—around 1.3 km (0.8 miles) deep—has a raised rim created by material thrown outward by the crash. The surrounding area is covered by paler material scattered across the surface.

Lava Seas

Known as maria (plural) and mare (singular) in Latin, seas were made when lava flowed from low volcanoes then cooled into the rock basalt. Huge eruptions filled wide impact craters. Volcanoes on Earth are usually caused by the movement of tectonic plates, but the Moon has no tectonic plates. Its eruptions were caused by super-hot magma welling up from the mantle. Most eruptions took place more than 1 billion years ago, when the Moon's interior was hotter than today.

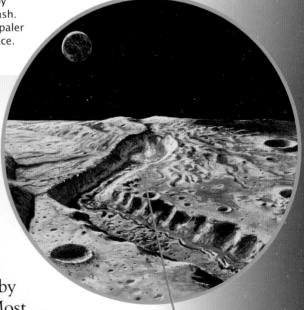

This illustration shows a volcano erupting on the Moon, its lava flowing into a valley known as Schroter's Valley. Such winding valleys, known as rilles, formed when old lava flows collapsed.

DID YOU KNOW? The Moon's largest crater is the far side's South Pole–Aitken Basin, which is 2,500 km (1,600 miles) across and around 4.2 billion years old.

OCEANUS PROCELLARUM PROFILE

Diameter: 2,592 km (1,611 miles)
Area: Around 4 million sq km (1.5 million sq miles)
Age: Around 1 billion years old
Named by: Italian astronomer Giovanni Battista Riccioli in 1651
Visited by: Crewed mission *Apollo 12* (1969) and robotic space probes *Luna 9* (1966), *Luna 13* (1966), *Surveyor 1* (1966), *Surveyor 3* (1967), and *Chang'e 5* (2020)

Mare Serenitatis
(Sea of Serenity)

Mare Imbrium
(Sea of Rain)

Mare Tranquillitatis
(Sea of Tranquillity)

Copernicus
Crater

Mare Crisium
(Sea of Crises)

Oceanus Procellarum (Ocean of Storms) is the largest of the Moon's seas and the only one called an "ocean."

The bright Tycho Crater, only 108 million years old, is just visible to the human eye from Earth.

Tides

Tides are the rise and fall of Earth's sea levels, resulting in ocean water moving up and down the shore each day. "High tide" is when the water reaches its highest point on the shore. Tides are caused by the gravitational pulls of the Moon and Sun as Earth rotates.

Pull of the Moon

The Moon's gravity makes the oceans bulge on the side of Earth facing the Moon. On the opposite side of Earth, where the Moon's pull is weakest, ocean water can flow away from Earth, creating another bulge. As Earth rotates, most places pass through both the ocean bulges each day, creating two high tides and two low tides. However, since the Moon does not orbit Earth exactly around the equator (and the continents also get in the way of tidal bulges), some places experience only one high tide each day.

Low tide leaves behind pools among coastal rocks, where animals such as crabs and prawns take shelter until the ocean returns.

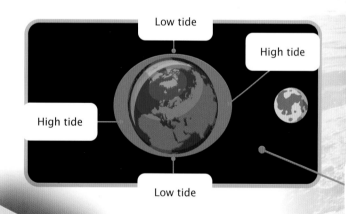

Low tide

High tide

High tide

Low tide

High tides occur on opposite sides of Earth.

GRAVITATIONAL PULLS

As felt on the object's surface

Sun: 28 times Earth's gravitational pull
Jupiter: 2.5 times Earth's gravitational pull
Saturn and Neptune: 1.1 times Earth's gravitational pull
Venus and Uranus: 0.9 times Earth's gravitational pull
Mercury and Mars: 0.38 times Earth's gravitational pull
Moon: 0.17 times Earth's gravitational pull

DID YOU KNOW? The Moon's gravity also creates bulges in Earth's crust, which can be measured using scientific instruments: New York City rises by 35 cm (14 in) at high tide.

The base of this rock has been worn away by waves up to the level of high tide.

The Moon rises above the horizon around 50 minutes later each day than the day before, so the times of high and low tides vary, making it essential to watch out for the rising tide.

Spring tides

Lunar tide

Solar tide

Neap tides

Pull of the Sun

The Sun also pulls on the oceans, but since it is much farther away than the Moon, its effect on tides is smaller. However, when the Sun and Moon are in a line, their combined gravity causes very high tides, known as spring tides. When the Sun and Moon are at right angles, the Sun works against the pull of the Moon, causing lower high tides and higher low tides, known as neap tides.

Spring and neap tides occur twice during each orbit of the Moon around Earth.

Watching the Moon

The side of the Moon facing the Sun is illuminated by sunlight. As the Moon orbits Earth, we can see different amounts of its sunlit side, making it appear to change shape in a cycle that lasts around 29.5 days.

Around 7 days before full moon, the Moon can be seen easily in the afternoon sky. Around 14 days later, it can be seen easily in the morning sky.

Phases of the Moon

When the Moon is on the opposite side of Earth from the Sun, we can see all its sunlit side. This phase is known as the full moon. When the Moon passes between Earth and the Sun, we can see none of its sunlit side. This phase is known as the new moon. Although it takes the Moon 27.3 days to orbit Earth, the Earth's own orbit around the Sun means that it takes around 29.5 days for the Moon to move through its phases.

First quarter

Full moon

New moon

Last quarter

Our view of the Moon changes as it orbits Earth.

LUNAR ECLIPSES OF 21ST CENTURY

Number: 230 (87 penumbral, 58 partial, and 85 total)
Most eclipses in a year: 4 (in 2009, 2020, 2038, 2085, 2096)
Most total eclipses in a year: 2
Longest duration of a total eclipse: 1 hour 46 minutes
Shortest duration of a total eclipse: 12 minutes

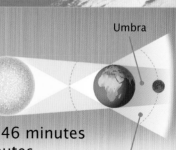

Umbra

Penumbra

During a total lunar eclipse, the Moon appears red because the only sunlight reaching its face has been bent by Earth's atmosphere. The Sun's blue light has been scattered by Earth's atmosphere, leaving only reddish light.

Eclipses of the Moon

An eclipse of the Moon, known as a lunar eclipse, is when the Moon moves into Earth's shadow, which can happen only at full moon. An eclipse does not happen every full moon because the Moon's orbit is tilted 5 degrees away from Earth's orbit around the Sun, so the Moon, Earth, and Sun are not always lined up. A total eclipse is when the Moon moves into the darkest part of Earth's shadow, the umbra. A penumbral eclipse is when it moves into the outer part of Earth's shadow, the penumbra, so its face dims. A partial eclipse is when part of the Moon's face enters Earth's umbra.

The Moon rises in the east and sets in the west.

The Moon spends around 12 hours out of every 24 hours above the horizon, some of those hours during the daytime. However, near new moon it is too close to the Sun's brightness to be seen during the day. When it is near full moon, it is visible only from the nighttime side of Earth.

DID YOU KNOW? On average, a total eclipse of the Moon happens every 2.5 years and can be seen from the nighttime side of Earth.

Chapter 3

The Inner Planets

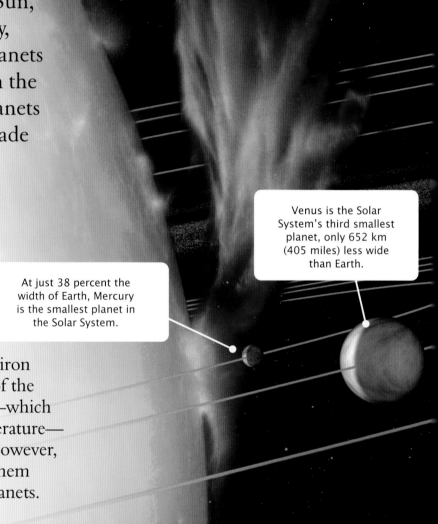

From closest to farthest from the Sun, the four inner planets are Mercury, Venus, Earth, and Mars. These planets are also known as terrestrial (from the Latin for "Earthlike") or rocky planets because—like Earth—they are made of rock with a metal core.

Earthlike Planets

The inner planets are made of heavier materials than the outer planets: Silicate rocks (made of minerals containing lots of silicon and oxygen atoms) form their mantles and crusts, while metals such as iron and nickel form their cores. In the heat of the inner solar system, only these materials—which do not melt until they reach a high temperature—can stay solid enough to make planets. However, the small size of the inner planets gives them lower masses (weights) than the outer planets.

At just 38 percent the width of Earth, Mercury is the smallest planet in the Solar System.

Venus is the Solar System's third smallest planet, only 652 km (405 miles) less wide than Earth.

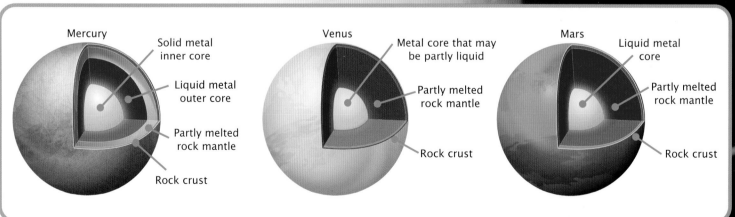

Mercury
- Solid metal inner core
- Liquid metal outer core
- Partly melted rock mantle
- Rock crust

Venus
- Metal core that may be partly liquid
- Partly melted rock mantle
- Rock crust

Mars
- Liquid metal core
- Partly melted rock mantle
- Rock crust

Too Small

Unlike the outer planets, the inner planets do not have ring systems. They also have fewer moons or no moons at all. This is largely because the inner planets' smaller masses give them weaker gravity than the outer planets—usually preventing them from capturing passing objects to become moons or holding on to rubble created by collisions.

Due to its immense size, which gives it great mass despite its light materials, Jupiter's gravity is 6.6 times the strength of Mercury's gravity.

Sun

Jupiter

Saturn

Uranus

Neptune

Venus

Mercury

Earth

Mars

The largest inner planet, Earth is the only one with flowing oceans, falling rainwater—and living things.

The second smallest planet, Mars has the most moons of any inner planet: two.

DID YOU KNOW? All the inner planets except Mercury have a thick enough atmosphere to create weather, caused by movements of gas.

Mercury

The Romans named Mercury after their fast-running messenger god, due to the planet's speedy motion. It orbits the Sun in just 88 days, moving at an average speed of 170,496 km/h (105,941 miles per hour), faster than any other planet.

Speedy Planet

Mercury has the fastest orbital speed because it is the closest planet to the Sun. The closer a planet is to the Sun, the faster it has to orbit so it is not pulled into the Sun by the star's immense gravity. The Sun is "trying" to pull all the planets into it, but they are "trying" to travel in a straight path. The balance between these two forces creates a curving path: an orbit.

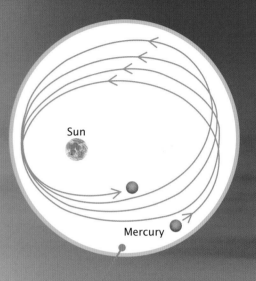

Sun

Mercury

Mercury's orbit is not a circle but an ellipse, ranging from 47 million to 70 million km (29 million to 43 million miles) from the Sun. The ellipse rotates over time.

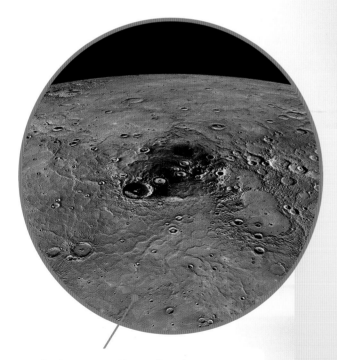

Dark craters at Mercury's poles stay so cold that they may hold water ice. This image captured by the *MESSENGER* space probe shows possible ice in yellow.

Hot and Cold

The surface temperature on Mercury varies more widely than on any other planet. During the daytime, the planet's closeness to the Sun heats it to 430 °C (800 °F). Mercury is too small and too close to the Sun for its gravity to hold on to more than an extremely thin atmosphere. With almost no atmosphere to blanket the planet and retain heat at night, the temperature can fall to -180 °C (-290 °F).

MERCURY PROFILE

Diameter: 4,880 km (3,032 miles)
Mass: 0.055 Earths
Average distance from the Sun: 57.9 million km (36 million miles)
Orbit: 88 days
Rotation: 59 days
Moons: 0

Since Mercury is visible to the naked eye as a bright, starlike object, it has been observed since ancient times.

The largest planet, Jupiter, is just about to set.

Mercury's closeness to the Sun means it can only be seen during twilight, near the western horizon shortly after sunset and near the eastern horizon just before sunrise.

DID YOU KNOW? Mercury rotates exactly three times on its axis for every two orbits it makes around the Sun, due to the Sun's intense gravity slowing its spin.

Mercurian Surface

Mercury has many thousands of impact craters, more than any other Solar System planet. Many craters and lowlands are flooded with dried lava that welled up from the interior when the planet was much hotter than today. The craters are crisscrossed by strange wrinkles called rupes.

Mercury's surfa...
is composed of ...
brown rock, but ...
photograph has ...
brighter shades ...
show the differe...
materials.

Craters

Mercury is more cratered than the other inner planets because it has little atmosphere to slow down asteroids and comets. Most of Mercury's craters were made within the first billion years after the planet's formation, when there were more stray space rocks than today. The smallest known craters are around 10 km (6 miles) wide, while the largest, the Caloris Basin, is 1,550 km (960 miles) across.

Taken by the *MESSENGER* space probe, this photo shows, at top right, the Brontë Crater (named after English authors Charlotte, Emily, Anne, and Bramwell Brontë) and the adjacent bluish Degas Crater (named after the French painter Edgar Degas).

CALORIS BASIN PROFILE

Diameter: 1,550 km (960 miles)
Area: Around 1.8 million sq km (700,000 sq miles)
Age: Around 3.9 billion years old
Discovered by: The *Mariner 10* space probe in 1974
Named after: The Latin for "heat" because the Sun is almost directly overhead every second time Mercury draws closest to the star

DID YOU KNOW? Mercury's rupes are named after ships used for expeditions o... including Charles Darwin's *Discovery* and Christopher Columbus's *Santa María*.

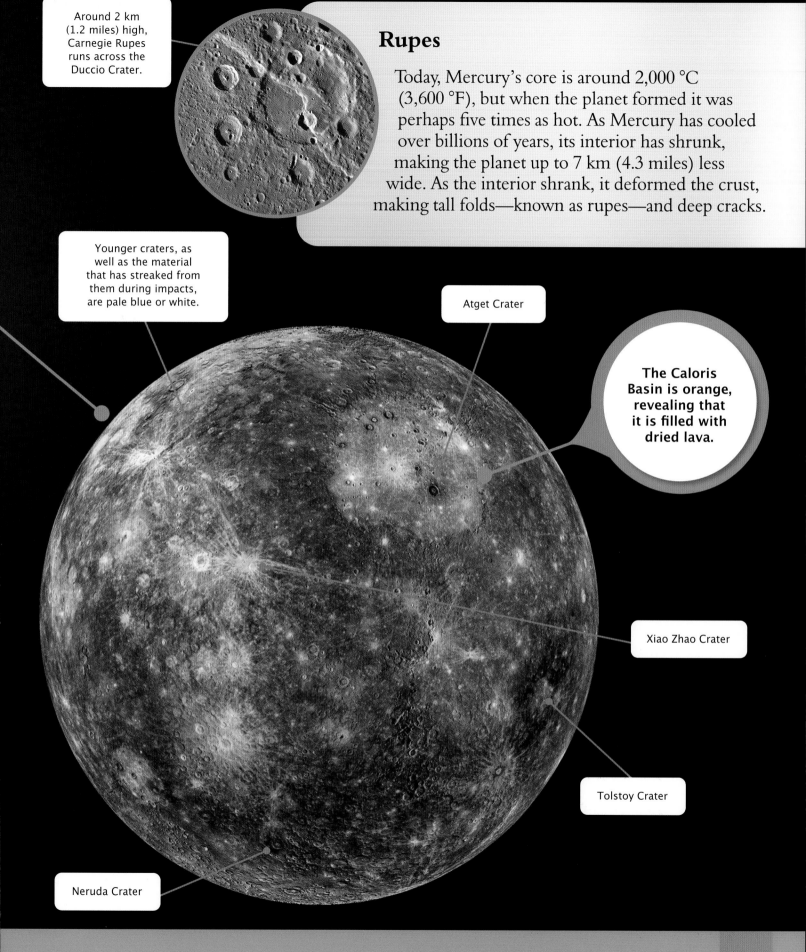

Around 2 km (1.2 miles) high, Carnegie Rupes runs across the Duccio Crater.

Rupes

Today, Mercury's core is around 2,000 °C (3,600 °F), but when the planet formed it was perhaps five times as hot. As Mercury has cooled over billions of years, its interior has shrunk, making the planet up to 7 km (4.3 miles) less wide. As the interior shrank, it deformed the crust, making tall folds—known as rupes—and deep cracks.

Younger craters, as well as the material that has streaked from them during impacts, are pale blue or white.

Atget Crater

The Caloris Basin is orange, revealing that it is filled with dried lava.

Xiao Zhao Crater

Tolstoy Crater

Neruda Crater

Venus

Named after the Roman goddess of love, Venus has been important to many cultures since ancient times, due to its bright appearance in the evening and morning sky. Today, it is often known as Earth's "sister planet" due to its similar size, mass, and composition.

Viewing Venus

Venus can be seen easily with the naked eye as a pale yellow light. It is the brightest object in the night sky apart from the Moon, because its thick clouds reflect much of the sunlight that reaches them. Unlike stars, Venus and the other planets do not appear to twinkle. Since Venus lies closer to the Sun than Earth, it always appears quite near our star. Yet, unlike Mercury, which is so near the Sun that it can be seen only in twilight, Venus can be seen for up to 3 hours before and after sunset and sunrise.

Like most features on Venus, Llorona Planitia (Llorona Plain) was named after a famous woman or a goddess, in this case a woman from Mexican legends.

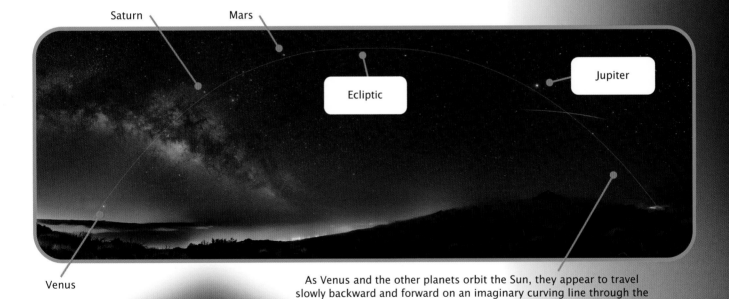

Saturn • Mars • Ecliptic • Jupiter • Venus

As Venus and the other planets orbit the Sun, they appear to travel slowly backward and forward on an imaginary curving line through the sky, known as the ecliptic. The ecliptic is the plane of the Solar System as seen from Earth, along which the Sun and Moon also appear to travel.

VENUS PROFILE

Diameter: 12,104 km (7,521 miles)
Mass: 0.815 Earths
Average distance from the Sun:
    108.2 million km (67.2 million miles)
Orbit: 224.7 days
Rotation: 243 days
Moons: 0

Turning Backward

Apart from Venus and Uranus, all the Solar System planets rotate counterclockwise (anticlockwise) on their axes as viewed from their north pole, the same direction in which they travel around the Sun. Venus rotates the opposite way on its axis, known as retrograde (backward) rotation. Venus must once have rotated the "right" way due to the way it formed in the Sun's spinning disk, but something—such as a crash with another planet—sent it spinning the other way, as was probably also the case with Uranus.

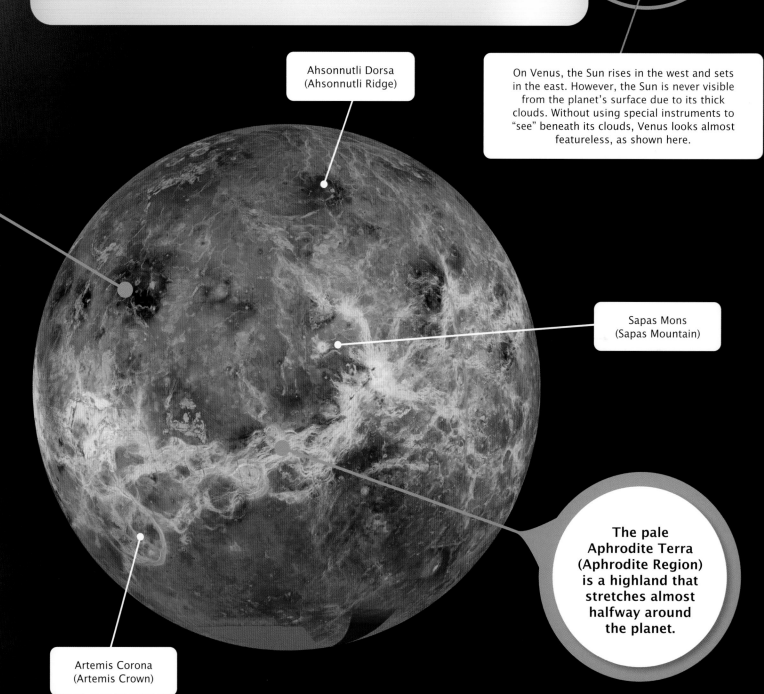

On Venus, the Sun rises in the west and sets in the east. However, the Sun is never visible from the planet's surface due to its thick clouds. Without using special instruments to "see" beneath its clouds, Venus looks almost featureless, as shown here.

Ahsonnutli Dorsa
(Ahsonnutli Ridge)

Sapas Mons
(Sapas Mountain)

The pale Aphrodite Terra (Aphrodite Region) is a highland that stretches almost halfway around the planet.

Artemis Corona
(Artemis Crown)

DID YOU KNOW? Venus rotates more slowly around its axis than any other planet, at 6.5 km/h (4 miles per hour) compared with Earth's 1,674 km/h (1,040 miles per hour).

Venusian Atmosphere

While Earth has an atmosphere that nurtures life, Venus's atmosphere would be deadly to all known life forms. The Venusian atmosphere also makes it the hottest planet in the Solar System, with an average surface temperature of 464 °C (867 °F).

A Deadly Mix

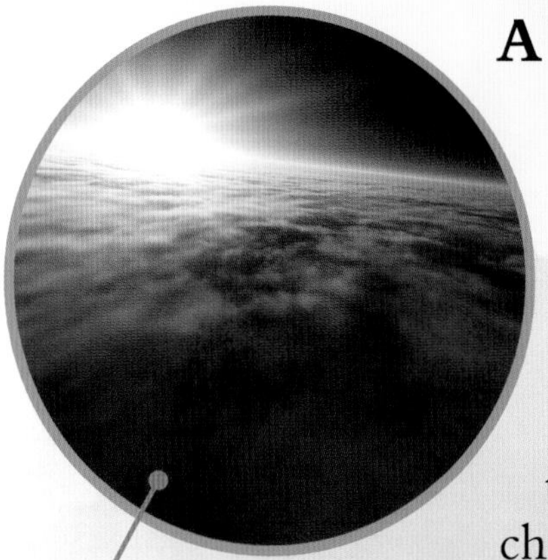

The Venusian atmosphere is extremely thick, with a mass 92 times Earth's atmosphere. If it were possible to stand safely on Venus's surface, the atmosphere would press down with the same weight felt 1 km (0.6 miles) underwater. The atmosphere is largely carbon dioxide, a gas that makes up less than 0.1 percent of Earth's atmosphere and would kill if breathed in such quantities. Venus's thick clouds are composed mainly of sulfuric acid, a dangerous chemical that—on Earth—is used to break down rocks and metals.

This illustration shows the top of Venus's yellowish cloud belt, which is always around 20 km (12.4 miles) thick.

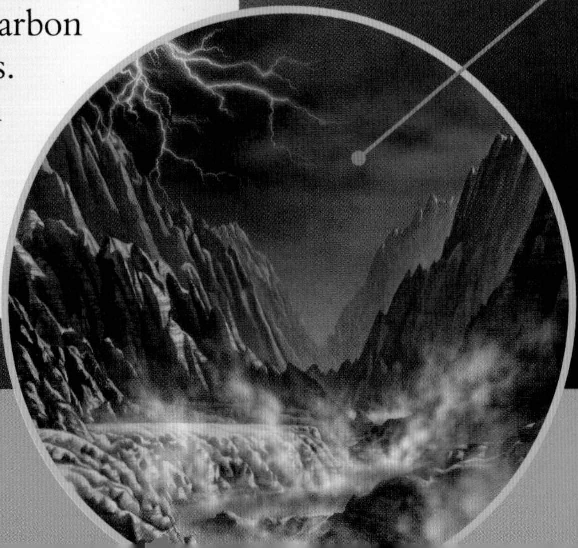

Venus's water boiled away as its temperature rose. Unfortunately, we are seeing a little of the same "global warming" effect on Earth, due to excess carbon dioxide released by cars and factories—but our planet is unlikely to become as hot as Venus.

Heating Up

Venus's intense heat is caused by the atmosphere's carbon dioxide, which traps the Sun's heat. Scientists think that, for the first 2 billion years of its life, Venus had less carbon dioxide in its atmosphere and lower temperatures. The carbon dioxide may have been released from the planet's interior. While today the Venusian surface is hot, dry rock, it might once have been cool enough for flowing oceans.

Venus's clouds may be able to generate lightning, as their droplets of sulfuric acid become electrically charged by rubbing together.

Although Venus's clouds produce sulfuric acid rain, the atmosphere's intense heat makes the drops evaporate (turn to gas) before reaching the surface.

The temperature on the surface would melt metals such as tin and lead.

GASES IN VENUS'S ATMOSPHERE

Carbon dioxide: Around 96.5 percent
Nitrogen: Around 3.5 percent
Sulfur dioxide, argon, water vapor, carbon monoxide, helium, and neon: Traces

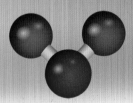

Each molecule of carbon dioxide has one carbon atom joined to two oxygen atoms.

DID YOU KNOW? There is little wind near Venus's surface, but above the clouds, winds can blow at 360 km/h (220 miles per hour).

Venusian Volcanoes

The *Magellan* space probe detected recent ash flows near the summit, suggesting that this volcano is still active.

With more than 1,600 major volcanoes, Venus has more volcanoes than any other Solar System planet. Two-thirds of the Venusian surface is covered by dried lava, which has concealed many impact craters—resulting in Venus having fewer than a thousand visible craters.

Making Volcanoes

On Earth, most volcanoes are caused by the movement of tectonic plates (see page 30), but Venus's crust and upper mantle are not broken into plates. Its volcanoes are caused by super-hot rock, known as magma, rising up from the mantle and through cracks in the crust. Such magma plumes also cause some Earth volcanoes, including those on the islands of Hawaii, in the Pacific Ocean. Although most Venusian volcanoes are probably inactive and we have never witnessed an eruption, astronomers think some are still active.

This overhead image of the volcano Sapas Mons, which is around 400 km (250 miles) wide, shows its twin dark summits. Paler areas are dried lava flows. In 2014, flashes caused by hot gas or lava were detected.

MAAT MONS PROFILE

Diameter: 395 km (245 miles)
Area: Around 122,500 sq km (47,000 sq miles)
Age: Probably less than 500 million years old
Discovered by: The *Pioneer Venus* space probe in 1978
Named after: The ancient Egyptian goddess of truth and justice, Maat, while "Mons" means mountain in Latin

DID YOU KNOW? Venus has 167 volcanoes over 100 km (60 miles) wide, while Earth has only one such volcano complex, on the Island of Hawaii in the Pacific Ocean.

Around 8 km (5 miles) tall, Maat Mons (Maat Mountain) is the highest volcano on Venus.

Volcano Types

Like most volcanoes on Earth, many volcanoes on Venus—including Maat and Sapas Mons—took the shape of mountains as dried lava built up. Other volcanoes have taken forms not seen on Earth:

Tick-like, or arachnoid, volcanoes are domes with numerous "legs," like the little bugs. These volcanoes may have formed when upwelling magma caused cracks to spread outward in the surface crust.

Crown-like, or corona, structures may have been made when a plume of magma pushed the crust upward into a dome, which then collapsed in the middle as the magma leaked out at the sides.

This radar image of Maat Mons was created by *Magellan* in 1991. A radar system sends out radio waves, then measures how long the waves take to bounce off surfaces and return. The shades of the image's yellow–brown rocks are based on photos taken by the *Venera 13* and *14* probes.

Mars

To the naked eye, Mars is a small reddish light, gaining it the nickname "Red Planet." Mars's shade reminded the ancient Romans of blood, so they named the planet after their god of war. Martian features were named after scientists, characters from myths, and Earth towns and rivers.

Red Planet

Mars's reddish shade is caused by the high quantity of iron oxide in its rocks and dust. Iron oxide, also known as rust, usually forms on Earth when iron is in contact with oxygen in the air, resulting in a flaky red coating. In addition to having a core of iron, nickel, and sulfur, Mars's surface rocks also contain large quantities of iron. Mars's atmosphere currently does not contain enough oxygen to rust its rocks, but possibly it once contained more—or perhaps oxygen in ancient water (see page 60) was responsible.

The *Curiosity* rover took this photo of Mars's rocky, sandy, dusty surface, as well as its own tracks.

This side-on view of Mars's atmosphere, photographed by *Viking 1*, shows a reddish haze of dust lifted into the air by wind.

Not Much of an Atmosphere

Mars has a very thin atmosphere, composed of 95 percent carbon dioxide, 2.8 percent nitrogen, 2 percent argon, and traces of oxygen and water. Earth's atmosphere is 100 times denser than the Martian atmosphere. Astronomers think that the Martian atmosphere was much denser in the past, but was stripped away by the solar wind (see page 22). Due to Mars having little atmosphere to retain heat—as well as its greater distance from the Sun—it is cooler than Earth, with the surface temperature averaging -60 °C (-76 °F).

DID YOU KNOW? In 2018, a Mars-wide dust storm destroyed the *Opportunity* rover, probably because dust got inside its equipment or covered its solar panels.

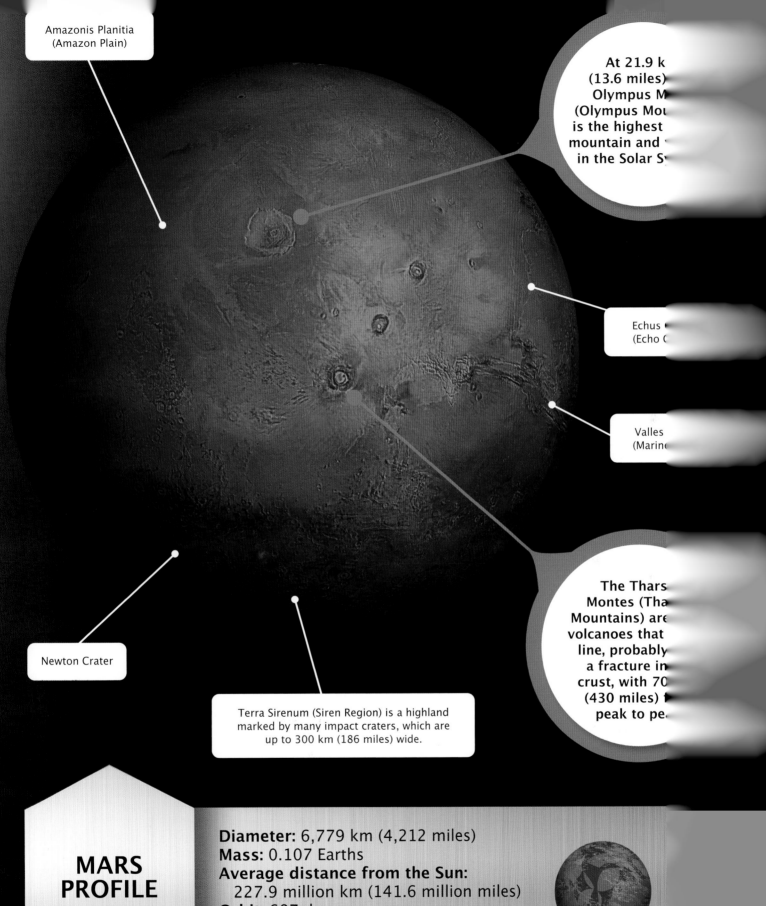

Amazonis Planitia
(Amazon Plain)

At 21.9 k
(13.6 miles)
Olympus M
(Olympus Mou
is the highest
mountain and
in the Solar S

Echus
(Echo C

Valles
(Marine

Newton Crater

Terra Sirenum (Siren Region) is a highland
marked by many impact craters, which are
up to 300 km (186 miles) wide.

The Thars
Montes (Tha
Mountains) are
volcanoes that
line, probably
a fracture in
crust, with 70
(430 miles)
peak to pe

MARS PROFILE

Diameter: 6,779 km (4,212 miles)
Mass: 0.107 Earths
Average distance from the Sun:
   227.9 million km (141.6 million miles)
Orbit: 687 days
Rotation: 1.02 days
Moons: 2

Water on Mars

Today, Mars is a dry and dusty planet, but astronomers think it may once have had flowing rivers and seas. Since life on Earth began in the oceans, scientists are excited by the idea that Mars could once have been home to life. No evidence of ancient life forms has yet been found.

Ancient Water

Currently, there is plenty of water on Mars, but it is frozen at the cold poles and in the soil. If all this ice melted, it would cover the planet in an ocean 35 m (115 ft) deep. Yet, today, Mars has too thin an atmosphere for liquid surface water. Without a thick atmosphere pressing down, surface water would either turn to gas or freeze into ice. However, astronomers think that, billions of years ago, the Martian atmosphere was thick enough—and warm enough—to allow liquid surface water.

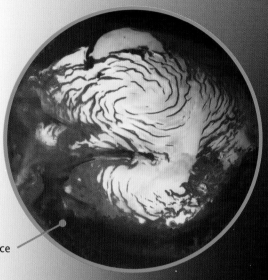

This photo, taken by the *Mars Express* space probe, shows ice at Mars's north pole.

Evidence of Water

Earth's surface has many features created by water erosion: the wearing away of rock by pounding waves and flowing rivers. Some of the same features can be found on Mars, providing possible evidence that the planet was once much wetter than it is now:

In this photo of the Eberswalde Crater, we can see a delta, a feature that forms on Earth where rivers enter lakes or seas. As the river meets the large body of slower-moving water, it drops the sand, gravel, and mud it is carrying, forming a fan shape.

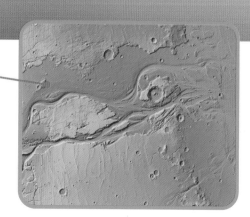

This map of the Kasei Valles (Kasei Valleys) uses different shades to show land heights, with yellow highest and blue lowest. The winding valleys, up to 3 km (1.9 miles) deep, may have been carved by rivers flowing toward a lake or sea on the right of the image.

Diameter: Around 1,000 km (620 miles) in summer
Volume of water ice: Around 821,000 cu km (197,000 cubic miles)
Age: Possibly around 1 billion years old
Discovered by: Italian astronomer Giovanni Cassini in 1666, but not identified as ice until 1719, by Giancomo Miraldi
First photographed from orbit by: The *Mariner 9* space probe in 1972

A large ocean may have covered one–third of the planet's surface.

Clouds could have drifted through the atmosphere, providing rain when their water droplets grew big and heavy.

This illustration imagines how Mars might have looked 4 billion years ago, when its atmosphere was thicker and warmer.

DID YOU KNOW? During every 687-day Martian year, each pole has around 300 days of continuous darkness during its winter, due to the planet's tilted axis.

Martian Canyons

Mars is home to one of the largest canyon systems in the Solar System: the Valles Marineris (Mariner Valleys). This series of cracks in the Martian crust was made by the growth of the Tharsis Bulge, a region of high ground that covers a quarter of the Martian surface.

Tharsis Bulge

Tharsis probably formed over an immensely hot region in the planet's mantle. Over billions of years, magma surged upward, pouring over the surface as runny lava—which built up a wide highland, more than 10 km (6.2 miles) higher than the planet's average surface. Three huge volcanoes also formed here, known as the Tharsis Montes (Tharsis Mountains): Ascraeus, Pavonis, and Arsia. The summit of the tallest, Ascraeus, is over 18 km (11 miles) high.

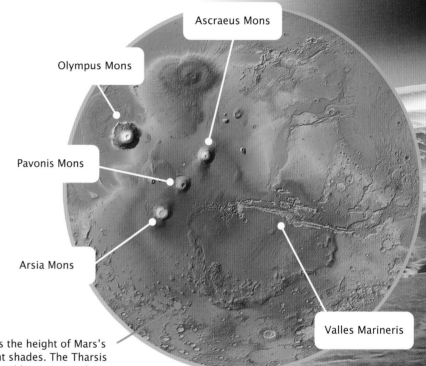

Ascraeus Mons

Olympus Mons

Pavonis Mons

Arsia Mons

Valles Marineris

This map shows the height of Mars's crust in different shades. The Tharsis Bulge (in red and brown) is in the middle, while the Valles Marineris (in blue) stretch to the east.

This image of the Valles Marineris was created using information collected by the *Mars Global Surveyor* space probe.

Valles Marineris

The Valles Marineris are a series of parallel canyons up to 8 km (5 miles) deep. In comparison, Earth's Grand Canyon is only 1.8 km (1.1 miles) deep. The cracks began to form around 3.5 billion years ago as Tharsis rose, causing the surrounding crust to stretch and break. As cracks opened, water that had been under the surface escaped, making the ground more unstable. The valleys' steep walls collapsed in landslides that widened the canyons yet more.

This illustration shows the central portion of the Valles Marineris, which are more than 4,000 km (2,485 miles) long in total.

The Candor Chasma (Candor Canyon) has been widened by wind, water, and landslides.

At 200 km (120 miles) wide, the Melas Chasma (Melas Canyon) is the widest portion of the canyon system.

VALLES MARINERIS PROFILE

Dimensions: Around 4,000 km (2,485 miles) long, 200 km (124 miles) wide, and up to 8 km (5 miles) deep
Age: Around 3.5 billion years old, with most canyon formation complete by 2 billion years ago
Discovered by: The *Mariner 9* space probe, the first probe to orbit another planet, in 1971
Named after: The *Mariner 9* space probe

DID YOU KNOW? Tharsis is named after the land of Tarshish, mentioned in the Bible and other ancient texts as a distant, faraway place.

Phobos and Deimos

Mars has two small moons named Phobos and Deimos. They were named after the twin sons of the Greek god of war, Ares, who was known to the Romans as Mars. Phobos ("fear" in ancient Greek) and Deimos ("dread") always followed their father onto the battlefield.

Phobos orbits closer to its parent planet than any other moon in the Solar System.

Mysterious Moons

Astronomers are not sure how Phobos and Deimos formed. Some think they were asteroids pulled in from the Asteroid Belt by Mars's gravity. Others think they formed when a larger moon was smashed by a passing object. Both moons are irregularly shaped because their own gravity is not powerful enough to pull them into a sphere.

Phobos orbits faster around Mars than the planet rotates, one of the few moons in the Solar System to do so. This means that, if it were possible to stand on the surface of Mars, Phobos would rise in the west, travel across the sky in 4 hours and 15 minutes or less, then set in the east, repeating this pattern around once every 11 hours and 6 minutes—twice each Martian day.

Deimos orbits slower around Mars than the planet rotates. Although it orbits in the same direction as Phobos—counterclockwise (anticlockwise), the same direction that Mars rotates—its slower motion means it rises in the east and sets in the west, the opposite of Phobos. A simple way to understand why is to imagine you (Mars) are running in a race. One person (Phobos) runs faster than you, so as they pass you their direction of travel appears to be forward. The other person (Deimos) runs slower than you, so as you pass them their direction of travel appears to be backward.

PHOBOS PROFILE

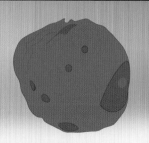

Diameter: 22.2 km (13.8 miles)
Mass: 0.0000000018 Earths
Average distance from Mars: 9,377 km (5,827 miles)
Orbit around Mars: 7.66 hours
Rotation: 7.66 hours

Diameter: 12.6 km (7.8 miles) across
Mass: 0.0000000002 Earths
Average distance from Mars:
 23,460 km (14,580 miles)
Orbit around Mars: 30.35 hours
Rotation: 30.35 hours

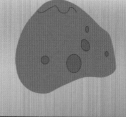

Viewed from Mars, Deimos would be so far away and so small that it would appear around one-twelfth the size of the Moon as seen from Earth.

Due to the pull of Mars's gravity, Phobos is getting nearer to the planet by 2 m (6.6 ft) every 100 years. In 30 to 50 million years, Phobos will draw so close it will be destroyed.

DID YOU KNOW? Mars's moons were discovered by American astronomer Asaph Hall in 1877, using the telescope at the US Naval Observatory.

The Outer Planets

From closest to farthest from the Sun, the four outer planets are Jupiter, Saturn, Uranus, and Neptune. Often known as the giant planets, they range in size from Neptune—almost four times the diameter of Earth—to Jupiter, which is eleven times wider than Earth.

Growing Giants

The inner planets are made of rock and metal, but the outer planets are made of materials called volatiles, such as hydrogen and methane. Volatiles turn to gas much more easily than rocks and metals. As the Solar System formed from the materials spinning around the young Sun, the heat in the Inner Solar System turned the volatiles to gas. The Sun's energy expelled the gassy volatiles into the Outer Solar System, where it was cool enough for them to form planets.

Uranus is the third largest Solar System planet, but it has the fourth biggest mass.

Jupiter

During the formation of the Solar System, there were far more volatile materials than rocky and metal materials spinning around the young Sun. This meant that the outer planets grew huge, but the inner planets are small.

Earth

DID YOU KNOW? The four outer planets make up 99 percent of the mass of all the objects known to orbit the Sun.

Jupiter's mass is 2.5 times the combined mass of all other objects orbiting the Sun.

Like all the outer planets, Neptune has a ring system and many moons.

The Solar System's second largest planet, Saturn is 9.5 times wider than Earth.

Gas or Ice?

Jupiter and Saturn are often known as gas giants, while Uranus and Neptune are called ice giants. These names are misleading, since all four planets are mostly swirling gas and liquid. Jupiter and Saturn are "gas" giants because they are mostly hydrogen and helium, which are gases at room temperature. Uranus and Neptune are "ice" giants because they are mostly water, ammonia, and methane, which freeze into ice at much higher temperatures than hydrogen and helium. For example, water freezes at 0 °C (32 °F), while hydrogen does not freeze until -259 °C (-434 °F).

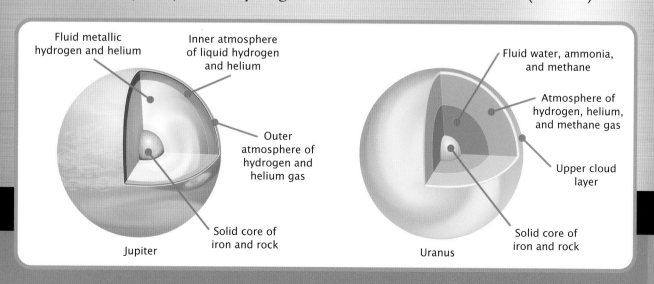

Fluid metallic hydrogen and helium

Inner atmosphere of liquid hydrogen and helium

Fluid water, ammonia, and methane

Atmosphere of hydrogen, helium, and methane gas

Outer atmosphere of hydrogen and helium gas

Upper cloud layer

Solid core of iron and rock

Jupiter

Solid core of iron and rock

Uranus

Jupiter

The Solar System's largest planet was named after the Roman king of the gods. At 4.6 billion years old, Jupiter is also the Solar System's oldest planet, perhaps 100 million years older than Earth. The planet has a faint ring system, composed of three rings of orbiting dust.

Jupiter's speedy spin, at nearly 45,000 km/h (28,000 miles per hour), has separated the planet's clouds into bands.

Seeing Jupiter

Saturn

Jupiter

Humans have observed Jupiter since ancient times as it is big and bright enough to be seen in the night sky without a telescope. It is visible for around eight months, followed by five months when it appears too close to the Sun to be seen from Earth. When visible, Jupiter is usually the third brightest object in the night sky, after the Moon and Venus. Since Jupiter's orbit is outside Earth's, it always appears nearly fully illuminated by the Sun's light.

When two planets appear close when viewed from Earth, it is known as a conjunction. In this photo, a conjunction of Jupiter and Saturn is to the left of the Milky Way Galaxy, which can be seen as a band of gas, dust, and stars.

The Great Red Spot

At the boundaries between Jupiter's belts and zones, where swiftly rising and falling gas meet, circling storms can form. Jupiter's biggest storm, known as the Great Red Spot, has been raging since at least 1831. It forms an orange area south of Jupiter's equator. Winds inside the storm are blowing at around 435 km/h (270 miles per hour) in a counterclockwise direction.

This photo of the Great Red Spot was taken in 1979 by the space probe *Voyager 1*. Since then, the storm has shrunk a little, to around 16,500 km (10,250 miles) across—still wider than Earth.

DID YOU KNOW? Jupiter's core has a temperature of around 19,700 °C (35,500 °F), but its surface is about −108 °C (−163 °F).

The light bands, called zones, are areas of warmer, rising gas that block our view of the orange gas below.

The dark bands, called belts, are regions of cooler, sinking gas containing chemicals stained orange by sunlight.

JUPITER PROFILE

Diameter: 139,822 km (86,881 miles)
Mass: 317.8 Earths
Average distance from the Sun:
  778 million km (484 million miles)
Orbit: 11.9 years
Rotation: 9.9 hours
Moons: 92 known

Moons of Jupiter

The largest of Jupiter's 92 known moons is Ganymede, the biggest moon in the Solar System. Among the smallest of the planet's moons is Valetudo, around 1 km (0.6 miles) across. Jupiter also has several smaller, unnamed moonlets, with perhaps many more still to be discovered.

Ganymede formed from the gas and dust spinning around Jupiter soon after the planet's birth.

Four Galilean Moons

Jupiter's four largest moons were the first objects discovered orbiting another planet. In 1609 or 1610, the Italian astronomer Galileo Galilei spotted them through his telescope. From closest to farthest from Jupiter, these moons are Io, Europa, Ganymede, and Callisto. The closer each moon is to the planet, the hotter its interior. This is due to Jupiter's gravity pulling on its rocks, creating heat from friction as they squeeze and bend.

Io		Around 421,700 km (262,032 miles) from Jupiter, Io is made of iron and rock with a sulfur surface. It has over 400 active volcanoes due to Jupiter's gravity melting its rock.
Europa		Cooler than Io, Europa has a metal core, a rocky mantle surrounded by an ocean of liquid salt water, and a thin crust of ice.
Ganymede		This moon has a metal core, a rocky mantle surrounded by an ocean of liquid salt water, and a thick crust of ice.
Callisto		Around 1,882,700 km (1,169,856 miles) from Jupiter, Callisto is a mix of rock and ice.

GANYMEDE PROFILE

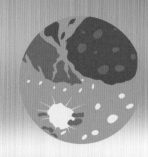

Diameter: 5,268 km (3,273 miles)
Mass: 0.025 Earths
Average distance from Jupiter: 1,070,400 km (665,116 miles)
Orbit around Jupiter: 7.13 days
Rotation: 7.13 days

Four Inner Moons

Four small moons orbit closer to Jupiter than the Galilean moons: Metis, Adrastea, Amalthea, and Thebe. The closest, Metis, is around 128,000 km (79,535 miles) from Jupiter. All the inner moons have irregular shapes because they are too small for their own gravity to pull them into a sphere. These moons shed material that keeps Jupiter's ring system supplied with dust.

Ganymede has countless craters, most of them caused by impacts with space rocks between 3.5 and 4 billion years ago.

Astronomers think there could be simple life forms in the ocean that lies beneath Ganymede's icy surface.

Jupiter's fifth largest moon, Amalthea is only 250 km (155 miles) long.

DID YOU KNOW? Jupiter's moons are named after lovers or children of the Roman god Jupiter or his Greek counterpart, Zeus.

Saturn

Like its sister planet Jupiter, Saturn is made mostly of hydrogen and helium. Although Saturn's great size gives it a mass 95 times Earth's, 1 cubic cm of Saturn would weigh only 0.7 g (0.02 oz), while the same quantity of Earth would weigh 5.5 g (0.2 oz).

Great White Spots

Around every 30 years, white thunderstorms encircle Saturn's northern hemisphere. They are named Great White Spots after Jupiter's Great Red Spot. The storms happen once every orbit, when Saturn's northern hemisphere is most tilted toward the Sun. They may be caused by rapidly rising hot gas. On Earth, quickly rising, hot, wet air causes thunderstorms.

Deep inside Saturn, hydrogen and helium gas are squeezed so tightly they become liquid and, deeper still, become metal.

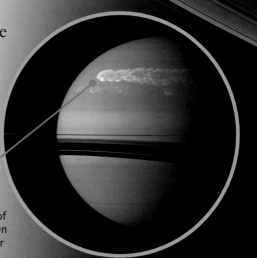

On Saturn, clouds are made of ammonia ice and water ice. On Earth, they are made of water ice or water droplets.

The Hubble Space Telescope took this photo of an aurora around Saturn's south pole.

Bright Lights

Space telescopes detect lights, known as auroras, around Saturn's poles. These are similar to the auroras seen on Earth (see page 36). Saturn has a magnetic field, possibly caused by electricity flowing inside the planet. A magnetic field is made when electricity is in motion. High-energy particles from the Sun are deflected by the magnetic field but hit near the polar regions where the field is weakest. The particles excite atoms of hydrogen gas, making them give off light.

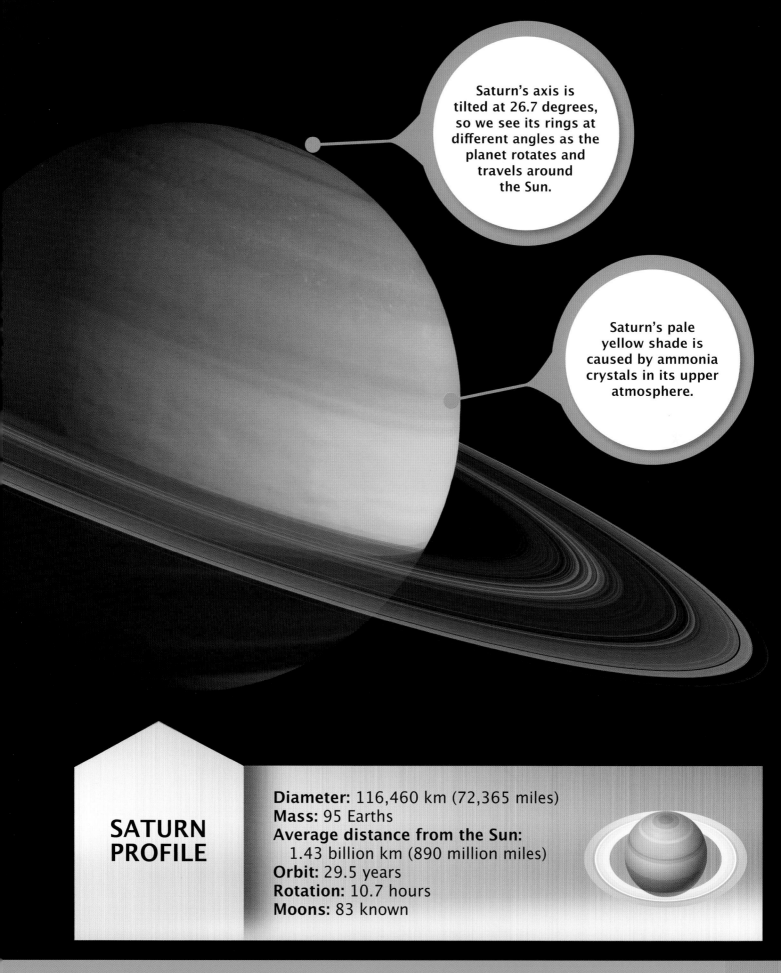

Saturn's axis is tilted at 26.7 degrees, so we see its rings at different angles as the planet rotates and travels around the Sun.

Saturn's pale yellow shade is caused by ammonia crystals in its upper atmosphere.

SATURN PROFILE

Diameter: 116,460 km (72,365 miles)
Mass: 95 Earths
Average distance from the Sun:
  1.43 billion km (890 million miles)
Orbit: 29.5 years
Rotation: 10.7 hours
Moons: 83 known

DID YOU KNOW? Astronomers think that it rains diamonds on Saturn after lightning turns the atmosphere's methane into carbon, which hardens into diamonds.

Rings of Saturn

Billions of chunks of almost pure water ice are orbiting Saturn. They form the Solar System's largest and brightest ring system, its brightness due to sunlight reflecting from the ice. The first person to see Saturn's rings was Galileo Galilei as he gazed through his telescope in 1610.

Around 4,800 km (3,000 miles) wide, the Cassini Division is a region between rings A and B where there is little material due to the moon Mimas sweeping it up.

Ring Structure

The main ring system contains rings named A to D. Rings A and B are the most tightly packed with material. Numerous gaps, where the material is sparser, lie between and among the rings. These gaps are caused by the gravitational pull of Saturn's moons and moonlets. Beyond ring A are several fainter, dustier rings, which extend as far as 13 million km (8 million miles) from Saturn.

The Encke Gap in the A ring is caused by the moon Pan, which orbits within it.

This image shows the rings in different shades depending on their particle size. Areas where most particles are larger than 5 cm (2 in) across are in purple, while green areas have lots of smaller particles.

SATURN'S RINGS PROFILE

Distance from Saturn's equator: 7,000 to 13 million km (4,300 to 8 million miles)
Thickness: 10 m to 1 km (33 ft to 0.6 miles)
Size of most particles: 1 cm to 10 m (0.4 in to 33 ft)
Mass: 0.0000026 Earths
Speed of orbit: 60,000 to 84,000 km/h (37,000 to 52,000 miles per hour)

If the rings formed from a shattered moon, the moon was probably 400 to 600 km (250 to 370 miles) across.

The B ring is the widest of the main rings, stretching for 25,500 km (15,845 miles).

Making Rings

Astronomers debate the age of Saturn's rings and how they formed. A common theory is that they formed between 10 million and 100 million years ago when one of the planet's moons was struck by a comet or asteroid. The moon shattered, making a cloud of rubble that was held in place by Saturn's gravity.

At first, the fragments would have been a jumbled cloud, but the gravity of Saturn and its moons produced a disk of fragments with circular orbits.

DID YOU KNOW? The Cassini Division was spotted in 1675 by Italian Giovanni Cassini. The astronomer also had a space probe to Saturn named after him in 1997.

Moons of Saturn

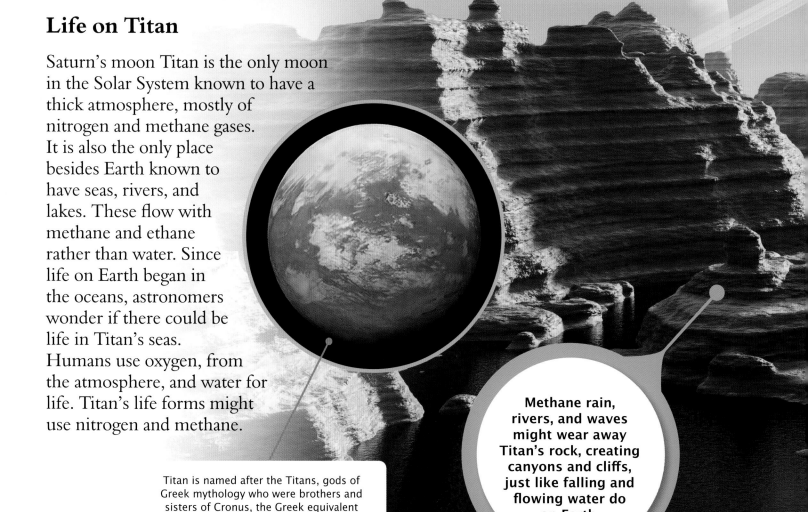

In this illustration, Titan's thick atmosphere makes the view of Saturn hazy.

Saturn has 83 known moons. Like the other giant planets, its great mass gives it immense gravity, so it can hold on to more moons than the inner planets. In addition, millions of unnamed smaller moonlets orbit within Saturn's rings.

Life on Titan

Saturn's moon Titan is the only moon in the Solar System known to have a thick atmosphere, mostly of nitrogen and methane gases. It is also the only place besides Earth known to have seas, rivers, and lakes. These flow with methane and ethane rather than water. Since life on Earth began in the oceans, astronomers wonder if there could be life in Titan's seas. Humans use oxygen, from the atmosphere, and water for life. Titan's life forms might use nitrogen and methane.

Titan is named after the Titans, gods of Greek mythology who were brothers and sisters of Cronus, the Greek equivalent of the Roman god of time, Saturn.

Methane rain, rivers, and waves might wear away Titan's rock, creating canyons and cliffs, just like falling and flowing water do on Earth.

DID YOU KNOW? The Solar System's largest moons are Jupiter's Ganymede, Saturn's Titan, Jupiter's Callisto and Io, Earth's Moon, and Jupiter's Europa.

TITAN PROFILE

Diameter: 5,149 km (3,200 miles)
Mass: 0.023 Earths
Average distance from Saturn: 1,221,870 km (759,235 miles)
Orbit around Saturn: 15.9 days
Rotation: 15.9 days

Titan is Saturn's largest moon. It is slightly bigger than the planet Mercury.

Contrasts on Iapetus

Around 1,469 km (913 miles) in diameter, Iapetus is Saturn's third largest moon, after Titan and Rhea. Iapetus is made of ice and rock. The moon puzzles astronomers by having one side that is light and one dark. The dark side is covered in a thin layer of a material that probably contains carbon, which is found in pencils and coal on Earth. The moon may have been spattered with this material by a nearby moon, such as Phoebe.

Iapetus is named after a Titan from Greek mythology, brother of Cronus, Rhea, and Phoebe.

Uranus

Only ever faintly visible to the naked eye, Uranus was believed to be a star until German-British astronomer William Herschel identified it as the Solar System's seventh planet in 1781. The planet's 13 dark, narrow rings were not discovered until 1977.

Methane in Uranus's atmosphere absorbs red light, making the planet look pale blue.

Turning Sideways

As the planets orbit the Sun, they also rotate around their own axis. Mercury, Venus, and Jupiter have an axis that points roughly "upward," at right angles to their journey around the Sun. Earth, Mars, Saturn, and Neptune have an axis that is tilted a little. Yet Uranus's axis is tilted over by 97.8 degrees, so it rotates on its side, with its ring system pointing upward. Astronomers think this tilt was created 3 to 4 billion years ago, when a planet larger than Earth crashed into Uranus.

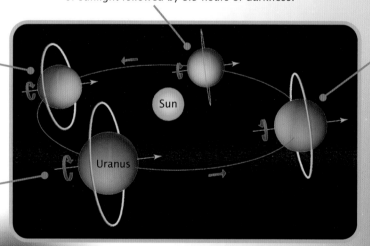

When Uranus's equator faces the Sun, for a brief period the planet has around 8.5 hours of sunlight followed by 8.5 hours of darkness.

Uranus's North Pole has nearly 42 years of sunlight, while its South Pole is in darkness.

Uranus's South Pole has nearly 42 years of sunlight, while its North Pole is in darkness.

Uranus's tilt gives the planet a strange pattern of night and day.

URANUS PROFILE

Diameter: 50,724 km (31,518 miles)
Mass: 14.5 Earths
Average distance from the Sun: 2.87 billion km (1.78 billion miles)
Orbit: 84 years
Rotation: 17.2 hours
Moons: 27 known

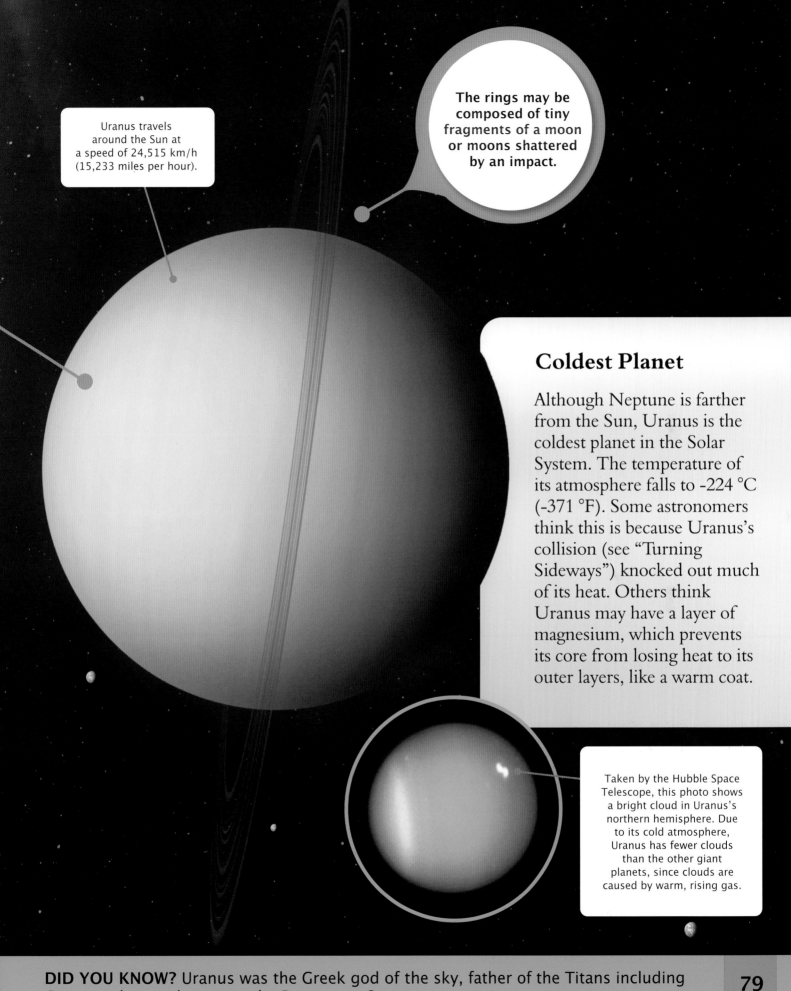

Uranus travels around the Sun at a speed of 24,515 km/h (15,233 miles per hour).

The rings may be composed of tiny fragments of a moon or moons shattered by an impact.

Coldest Planet

Although Neptune is farther from the Sun, Uranus is the coldest planet in the Solar System. The temperature of its atmosphere falls to -224 °C (-371 °F). Some astronomers think this is because Uranus's collision (see "Turning Sideways") knocked out much of its heat. Others think Uranus may have a layer of magnesium, which prevents its core from losing heat to its outer layers, like a warm coat.

Taken by the Hubble Space Telescope, this photo shows a bright cloud in Uranus's northern hemisphere. Due to its cold atmosphere, Uranus has fewer clouds than the other giant planets, since clouds are caused by warm, rising gas.

DID YOU KNOW? Uranus was the Greek god of the sky, father of the Titans including Cronus, who was known to the Romans as Saturn.

Moons of Uranus

The five largest of Uranus's 27 known moons were discovered between 1787 and 1948. The smaller moons were spotted in photos taken by the space probe *Voyager 2* in 1986, or were identified between 1997 and 2003 using advanced telescopes such as the Hubble Space Telescope.

Moon Groups

Orbiting among Uranus's rings are 13 small moons, none bigger than 162 km (100 miles) wide. Made of ice and an unknown dark material, these inner moons probably formed from the same shattered moon as the rings. Beyond the inner moons are five large moons, orbiting 129,390 to 583,520 km (80,400 to 362,580 miles) from Uranus. Far beyond the large moons are another nine small moons, which orbit up to 20.4 million km (12.7 million miles) from Uranus. These outer moons were probably objects captured by Uranus's gravity.

From Titania, Uranus appears around 13 times bigger in the sky than the Moon appears from Earth.

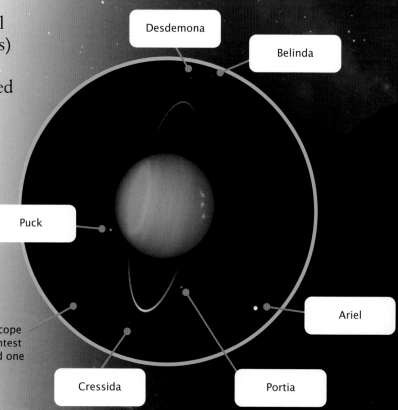

Desdemona

Belinda

Puck

Ariel

Cressida

Portia

In 2003, the Hubble Space Telescope took this photo of Uranus's brightest rings, five of its inner moons, and one of its large moons, Ariel.

TITANIA PROFILE

Diameter: 1,577 km (980 miles)
Mass: 0.00059 Earths
Average distance from Uranus: 435,910 km (270,860 miles)
Orbit around Uranus: 8.7 days
Rotation: 8.7 days

DID YOU KNOW? Uranus's moons are named after characters in the works of English playwright William Shakespeare and English poet Alexander Pope.

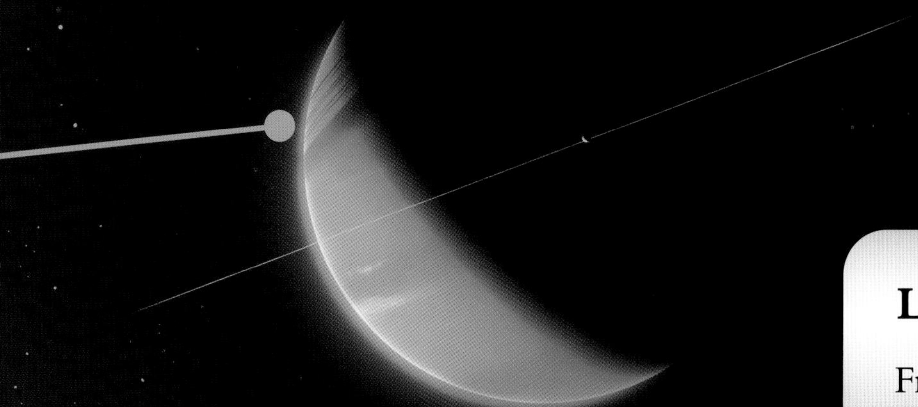

Large Moons

From biggest to smallest, Uranus's five large moons are: Titania, Oberon, Umbriel, Ariel, and Miranda. They probably formed from the gas and dust spinning around the young Uranus. Apart from Miranda, which is mostly ice, they are a mix of roughly equal parts rock and ice. Their surfaces are cratered by impacts with space rocks. All five make almost perfect circles around Uranus's dramatically tilted equator.

Miranda

Ariel

Umbriel

Titania

Oberon

Miranda is closest to Uranus's equator, while Oberon is farthest away.

The Solar System's eighth largest moon, Titania's surface has canyons and ridges caused by the moon expanding and cracking during its early life.

Neptune

Invisible to the naked eye, Neptune was the last of the eight planets to be discovered. A deeper blue than Uranus, Neptune gets its hue from methane and an unknown material in its atmosphere. Neptune has five main rings, which are very faint and dusty.

A Team Effort

In the early 19th century, French astronomer Alexis Bouvard realized there must be an undiscovered eighth planet when he noted that Uranus's orbit was affected by the pull of a more distant, large object. The French astronomer and mathematician Urbain Le Verrier then calculated where an eighth planet should be. He sent his findings to German astronomer Johann Galle, who found the new planet, soon named Neptune, through a telescope in 1846.

Urbain Le Verrier used mathematics to locate Neptune, which was the only one of the eight Solar System planets not found by sight alone.

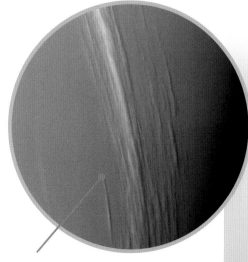

Taken by *Voyager 2*, this photo shows clouds of frozen methane crystals, which are parallel with Neptune's equator.

Windy Planet

Neptune has the fastest winds of any planet in the Solar System, blowing at up to 2,100 km/h (1,300 miles per hour). The super speed of these winds, which usually blow in the opposite direction to Neptune's rotation, is partly caused by Neptune's fast spin of 9,650 km/h (5,995 miles per hour). In addition, the winds are given energy by the planet's internal heat, which reaches 5,100 °C (9,200 °F) at Neptune's core.

DID YOU KNOW? Due to Neptune's great distance, the space probe *Voyager 2* is the only spacecraft that has flown past the planet.

The Great Dark Spot was an immense storm, recorded in this photo by *Voyager 2* in 1989, that had disappeared by 1994.

This patch of cloud was named Scooter due to its speed: It circled the planet every 16 hours.

A smaller storm, the Small Dark Spot, was around 6,280 km (3,900 miles) across.

NEPTUNE PROFILE

Diameter: 49,244 km (30,598 miles)
Mass: 17.1 Earths
Average distance from the Sun:
  4.5 billion km (2.8 billion miles)
Orbit: 164.8 years
Rotation: 16 hours
Moons: 14 known

Moons of Neptune

Neptune was the Roman god of the sea, so all the planet's 14 known moons are named after Greek and Roman gods, goddesses, and creatures linked with water. The largest moon, Triton, has a mass more than 500 times greater than the second largest moon, Proteus.

Seven Strange Moons

Neptune's outer moons are Triton, Nereid, Halimede, Sao, Laomedeia, Psamathe, and Neso. These moons have irregular orbits, which means that their path is very elliptical (stretched) and is inclined (tilted) rather than around the planet's equator. Four of them orbit in the opposite direction from the way their planet is turning. All this tells astronomers that the outer moons did not form around Neptune but were objects captured by the planet's gravity.

Triton was discovered by English astronomer William Lassell in 1846, 17 days after the discovery of Neptune.

Triton has a core of metal and rock, surrounded by frozen water and covered with frozen nitrogen.

Orbit of inner moon Proteus

Triton has an irregular orbit and travels in the opposite direction from Neptune's inner moons.

TRITON PROFILE

Diameter: 2,710 km (1,680 miles)
Mass: 0.0036 Earths
Average distance from Neptune: 354,800 km (220,500 miles)
Orbit around Neptune: 5.88 days
Rotation: 5.88 days

Around 420 km (260 miles) across, Proteus was photographed by the space probe *Voyager 2*.

Triton's surface erupts plumes of nitrogen gas and dust 8 km (5 miles) high, probably caused by the Sun heating nitrogen.

Larissa

Galatea

Taken by the Hubble Space Telescope, this photo shows Neptune with its four largest inner moons.

Despina

Seven Regular Moons

Neptune's seven inner moons are Naiad, Thalassa, Despina, Galatea, Larissa, Hippocamp, and Proteus. They probably formed when Triton was dragged into orbit, smashing Neptune's existing moons. Neptune's gravity pulled the rubble into orbit around its equator, spinning in the same direction the planet turned. The rubble clumped together, forming seven moons with regular orbits.

DID YOU KNOW? The Solar System's seventh largest moon, Triton was probably a dwarf planet pulled from the Kuiper Belt by Neptune's gravity.

Chapter 5

Other Solar System Objects

In addition to the eight planets and their moons, many trillions of smaller objects—made of rock, metal, dust, or ice—are in orbit around the Sun. The largest are known as dwarf planets, while the smallest are specks of dust in vast clouds.

Types of Objects

Some small Solar System objects, including comets and centaurs (see page 98), travel between different regions of the Solar System. However, most small objects orbit the Sun in distinct regions. Between the orbits of Mars and Jupiter, the Asteroid Belt contains objects known as asteroids, made of rock and metal. Beyond the orbit of Neptune, the Kuiper Belt and Scattered Disk hold objects made mostly of ice and rock. In the farthest regions of the Solar System are "detached objects" and the possible Oort Cloud.

Although most asteroids orbit in the Asteroid Belt, some—known as trojans—share the orbit of a planet or moon. Most trojans share the orbit of Jupiter.

This illustration compares the size of Earth with the three largest widely agreed dwarf planets, Pluto, Eris, and Haumea.

Dwarf Planets

Unlike a moon, a dwarf planet orbits the Sun directly. It has a mass (weight) large enough for its gravity to pull it into a rounded shape, which tends to happen when a rocky object is over 600 km (370 miles) wide. Yet a dwarf planet's gravity is not enough to clear objects out of its orbit, unlike a true planet. Different astronomers count different numbers of dwarf planets, from 5 to over 120. Most agree on 9: Ceres, in the Asteroid Belt; Orcus, Pluto, Haumea, Quaoar, and Makemake in the Kuiper Belt; Gonggong and Eris in the Scattered Disk; and the detached object Sedna.

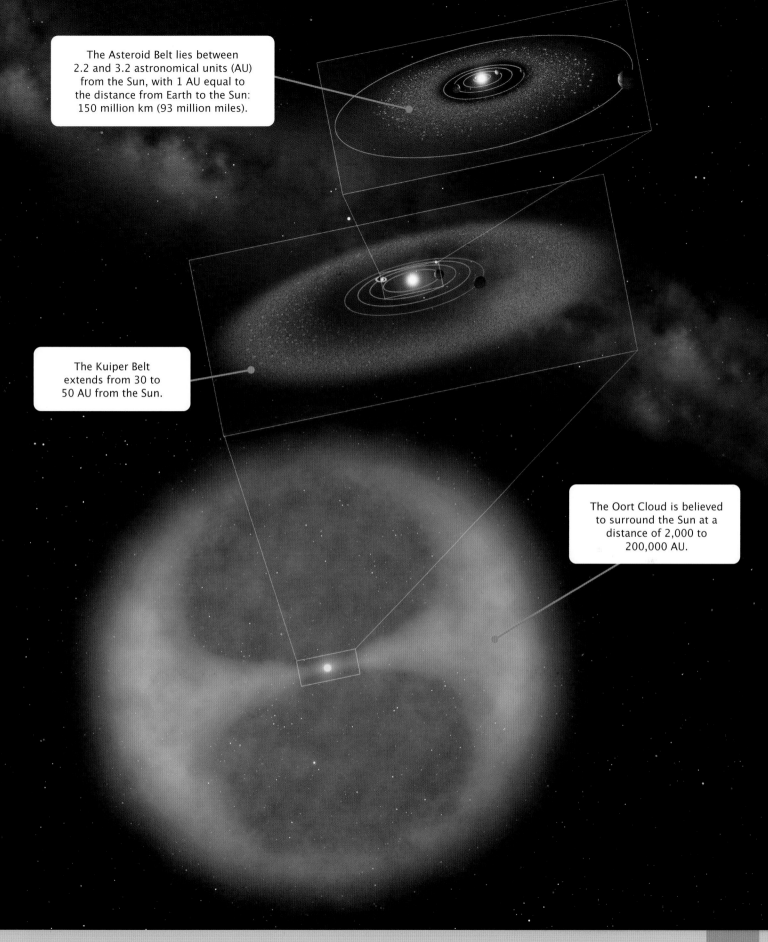

The Asteroid Belt lies between 2.2 and 3.2 astronomical units (AU) from the Sun, with 1 AU equal to the distance from Earth to the Sun: 150 million km (93 million miles).

The Kuiper Belt extends from 30 to 50 AU from the Sun.

The Oort Cloud is believed to surround the Sun at a distance of 2,000 to 200,000 AU.

DID YOU KNOW? Pluto was called a planet until 2006, when the International Astronomical Union put it in the newly defined category of dwarf planets.

Asteroid Belt

The Asteroid Belt contains up to 1.9 million asteroids larger than 1 km (0.6 miles) across and many millions of smaller ones. Asteroids are rocky and metallic objects left over from the formation of the Inner Solar System.

> The combined mass of all the asteroids in the Asteroid Belt is around 4 percent of the mass of Earth's Moon.

Forming the Belt

As the Solar System formed 4.6 billion years ago, the powerful gravity of nearby Jupiter disrupted the material in the Asteroid Belt region, keeping it from clumping together into a true planet. Asteroids are made of similar materials to the inner planets. Most are made of silicate rocks (like Earth's mantle and crust), while others contain large amounts of the metals nickel and iron (like Earth's core). Asteroids are in three main types, based on their composition:

C–type asteroid: Around 50 km (31 miles) across, Mathilde is made mainly of clay (an earthy material that forms in water) and silicate rocks.

S–type asteroid: About 12 km (7.5 miles) wide, Gaspra is made mainly of silicate rocks and nickel–iron.

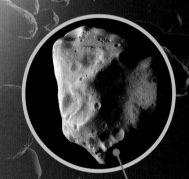

M–type asteroid: Lutetia, around 100 km (62 miles) across, contains high quantities of metal.

ASTEROID BELT PROFILE

Diameter: Around 150 million km (93 million miles)
Mass: 0.0048 Earths
Distance from the Sun: 329 million to 478.7 million km 204.4 million to 297.5 million miles)
Orbit of each asteroid: 3 to 6 years
Rotation of each asteroid: Up to 50 days

DID YOU KNOW? The four largest asteroids—Ceres, Vesta, Pallas, and Hygeia—account for around half the mass of the Asteroid Belt.

Each asteroid travels around the Sun in an elliptical orbit, while rotating—sometimes in a tumbling, disordered fashion—at the same time.

Asteroid Moons

More than 300 asteroids are orbited by their own small moon, some of them by two or three moons. The moons usually form when one asteroid hits another, breaking off a chunk that is held in orbit around the larger asteroid by its gravity. When the two broken chunks are of similar size, the two asteroids can orbit a point in space— where their masses are in balance—that lies between them. These asteroid pairs are known as double asteroids.

Most asteroids are irregularly shaped and cratered by impacts.

The asteroid Ida, with an average width of 31.4 km (19.5 miles), is orbited by the moon Dactyl, which is just 1.4 km (0.9 miles) across.

Ceres

Orbiting in the middle of the Asteroid Belt, Ceres is the only asteroid large enough to be considered a dwarf planet. It was the first object in the Asteroid Belt to be spotted, in 1801 by Italian astronomer Giuseppe Piazzi, who named it after the Roman goddess of farming.

Watery Rock

Ceres has the most water of any object in the Solar System apart from Earth. Around 25 to 50 percent of Ceres is water, which is mixed with rock, salty minerals, and clay. Since Ceres is cold, the water is almost completely frozen, but pockets of liquid water are believed to lie beneath the surface. Scientists wonder if tiny life forms might be found in this water.

Much of what we know about Ceres was discovered by the *Dawn* space probe, the first probe to orbit a dwarf planet, in 2015.

Ahuna Mons probably formed in the last 240 million years but is no longer active.

Ice Volcano

Ceres has one large mountain, Ahuna Mons, which is about 4 km (2.5 miles) high. It is a cryovolcano—an ice volcano. The mountain lies almost exactly on the opposite side of Ceres to the dwarf planet's largest impact crater, the Kerwan Basin, which measures 284 km (176 miles) across. The impact that made the crater may have broken the crust on the opposite side of Ceres, from which icy, muddy water erupted. The muddy water then froze, creating a mountain.

DID YOU KNOW? With binoculars or a store-bought telescope, Ceres is just bright enough to be seen in the night sky, looking like a dim star.

Far from the Sun, Ceres has a surface temperature between −163 and −38 °C (−261 and −36 °F).

Bright spots in Occator Crater are probably caused by icy salts reflecting the Sun's light.

Ceres has no atmosphere, apart from small amounts of water vapor (water in the form of a gas) that drift from the surface.

CERES PROFILE

Diameter: 939 km (583 miles)
Mass: 0.00016 Earths
Average distance from the Sun:
    414 million km (257 million miles)
Orbit: 4.6 years
Rotation: 9 hours
Moons: 0

Kuiper Belt

Beyond Neptune, the Kuiper Belt is a ring of icy objects that orbit the Sun. The Kuiper Belt is 20 times wider than the Asteroid Belt and contains around 20 times more material. There may be 100,000 Kuiper Belt objects (KBOs) more than 100 km (62 miles) wide.

Discovering the Kuiper Belt

The first KBO to be discovered was the largest, Pluto (see page 94), in 1930. Apart from Pluto and its largest moon, there was no proof of other objects beyond Neptune until 1992, when a third object was discovered—named Albion—by David Jewitt and Jane Luu, using a telescope at the Mauna Kea Observatory in Hawaii. Over 2,000 KBOs have been discovered since.

The Mauna Kea Observatory lies on a volcano summit, where the view of space is not obscured by pollution and clouds.

Not a Sphere

The second largest object in the Kuiper Belt is the dwarf planet Haumea, which measures around 2,000 km (1,245 miles) at its longest point. Unlike the other large dwarf planets, Haumea is not a sphere or close to one: It is an ellipsoid (a flattened sphere). Haumea's gravity was powerful enough to pull it into a rounded shape, but its very rapid rotation—of just 4 hours— flattened it, like a spinning ball of dough forms a pizza base.

Named after the Hawaiian goddess of childbirth, Haumea has two moons— Hi'iaka and Namaka, both also named after Hawaiian goddesses—as well as a ring of icy dust.

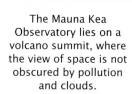

KBOs are made of rock and materials such as water, methane, and ammonia, which are frozen due to the average temperature of −220 °C (−364 °F).

KUIPER BELT PROFILE

Diameter: Around 3 billion km (1.9 billion miles)
Mass: Around 0.1 Earths
Distance from the Sun: 4.5 billion to 7.5 billion km
  (2.8 billion to 4.7 billion miles)
Orbit of each KBO: Around 200 to 320 years
Rotation of each KBO: Usually less than 1 day

This illustration imagines the moment when the *New Horizons* space probe flew past the KBO Arrokoth in 2019.

Arrokoth is formed of two KBOs that have joined together, resulting in a peanut-shaped object 36 km (22 miles) long.

DID YOU KNOW? The Kuiper Belt is named after Dutch astronomer Gerard Kuiper, who in 1951 suggested that there might be objects beyond Pluto.

Pluto

Orbiting in the Kuiper Belt, Pluto is the largest dwarf planet by diameter. Pluto was named after the Greek god of the underworld, a suggestion made by 11-year-old English schoolgirl Venetia Burney in 1930.

Pluto's Structure

Pluto has a large core of rock that takes up around two-thirds of its interior. The core is surrounded by a layer of water up to 180 km (112 miles) thick. The water is probably frozen, but some astronomers think Pluto's interior is warm enough for it to be liquid. Pluto's crust is made of frozen nitrogen (a gas that forms the majority of Earth's atmosphere), with traces of frozen water, methane, and carbon monoxide.

This photo of Pluto, taken by the *New Horizons* probe in 2015, has slightly exaggerated the shades of the planet's surface to show its different materials.

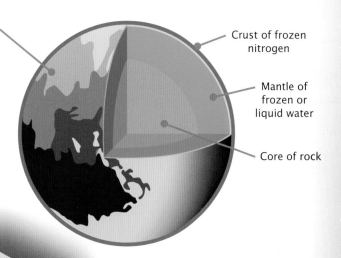

Pluto's core may be around 700 °C (1,292 °F), but its surface temperature is about –229 °C (–380 °F).

Crust of frozen nitrogen

Mantle of frozen or liquid water

Core of rock

Red areas are covered in an unknown material that may be created by sunlight heating the surface's methane and carbon monoxide, turning them red.

PLUTO PROFILE

Diameter: 2,377 km (1,477 miles)
Mass: 0.00218 Earths
Average distance from the Sun: 5.9 billion km (3.7 billion miles)
Orbit: 248 years
Rotation: 6.4 days
Moons: 5 known

DID YOU KNOW? Snow is rare in the Solar System, but when Pluto journeys farthest from the Sun, its thin atmosphere—which is mainly nitrogen gas—freezes and falls as snow.

Monster Moons

Pluto has five moons, all named after monsters or characters and places associated with the underworld in Greek myths. From closest to farthest from Pluto, they are: Charon, Styx, Nix, Kerberos, and Hydra. The largest moon, Charon, is around 1,212 km (753 miles) wide. It is so big compared with Pluto that the two objects orbit around a point in space a little outside Pluto. This has led some astronomers to call the pair a double dwarf planet.

Pluto

Charon

Pluto and Charon orbit a point 2,126 km (1,321 miles) from the middle of Pluto, where the two objects' masses are balanced.

Tombaugh Regio (Tombaugh Region) is a pale area of smooth, frozen nitrogen.

Scattered Disk

Like the Asteroid and Kuiper Belts, the Scattered Disk is a region of small objects that orbit the Sun. Yet Scattered Disk objects (SDOs) have more irregular orbits than the objects in the belts. Although the inner edge of the Scattered Disk overlaps with the Kuiper Belt, its outer edge is twice as far from the Sun.

Eris

The largest object in the Scattered Disk is Eris, which was discovered in 2005 and at first named a "planet" but soon downgraded to "dwarf planet." With a mass of around 0.0028 Earths, Eris is the biggest dwarf planet by mass, but—at 2,326 km (1,445 miles) across—it is slightly smaller than Pluto by diameter. Eris's greater mass is probably due to a larger quantity of rocky materials.

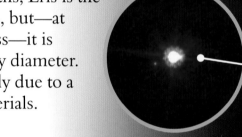

The Sun is an average 10 billion km (6.2 billion miles) from Eris, which rarely passes closer to another SDO (apart from its moon) than a million kilometers.

No space probe has yet taken close-up photos of Eris, but this image of the dwarf planet and its one known moon, Dysnomia, was captured by the Hubble Space Telescope in 2007.

Scattering

Like Kuiper Belt objects (KBOs), SDOs are made of frozen materials such as water and methane, as well as rock. SDOs probably once orbited in the Kuiper Belt, but they have been "scattered" by the gravity of Neptune. This made their orbits much more elliptical (stretched out of a circle). The scattering also tilted the SDOs' orbits away from the plane of the Solar System by up to 40 degrees, so they orbit both far above and below the Sun's equator.

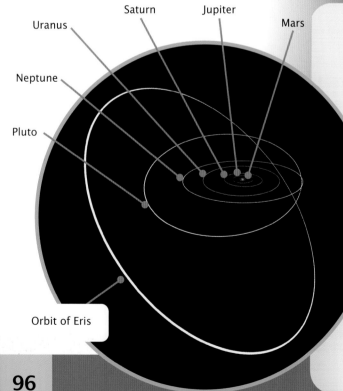

Uranus
Saturn
Jupiter
Mars
Neptune
Pluto

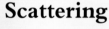
Orbit of Eris

This illustration shows Eris's orbit in comparison with the orbits of the planets and the KBO Pluto. Eris's average distance from the Sun is 68 AUs, but it travels as close as 38 AUs and as far as 97 AUs.

Diameter: Around 10.5 billion km (6.5 billion miles)
Mass: Between 0.01 and 0.1 Earths
Distance from the Sun: 4.5 billion to 15 billion km (2.8 billion to 9.3 billion miles)
Orbit of each SDO: Around 400 to 700 years
Rotation of each SDO: Usually less than 1 day

Eris's moon Dysnomia is about 700 km (435 miles) across, making it the 17th largest known moon in the Solar System.

This illustration imagines Eris with a pale crust, probably made of methane that is frozen due to a surface temperature of around −231 °C (−384 °F).

DID YOU KNOW? Eris was named after the Greek goddess of disagreement, since its discovery started a debate about the difference between a planet and dwarf planet.

97

Comets

Comets are rocky, dusty, icy objects with elliptical orbits that take them both close to and very far from the Sun. When comets near the Sun, they get so hot they release glowing gas. In most years, a comet can be seen—perhaps faintly—in the night sky without a telescope.

Making a Comet

Comets with orbits less than 200 years, known as short-period comets, probably started life in the Kuiper Belt or Scattered Disk. The gravity of the outer planets disturbed these objects, throwing them into highly elliptical orbits. Long-period comets, which have orbits between 200 and many thousands of years, may have begun in the Oort Cloud when a passing star disrupted their orbit. Centaurs are comet-like objects, probably from the Kuiper Belt, with orbits that cross the paths of the outer planets until they are thrown aside or destroyed.

The orbit of the long–period comet Hale–Bopp takes around 2,400 years. The spectacular comet was visible to the naked eye from Earth between 1996 and 1997.

Two Tails

The core of a comet, known as the nucleus, is made of rock, dust, water ice, and frozen gasses such as carbon monoxide and methane. When a comet passes the orbit of Jupiter, it thaws and starts to release gas. By the time the comet is passing Earth's orbit, it is trailing a tail of gas, which is always blown away from the Sun by the solar wind. As the comet nears the Sun, a second tail—made of dust—develops.

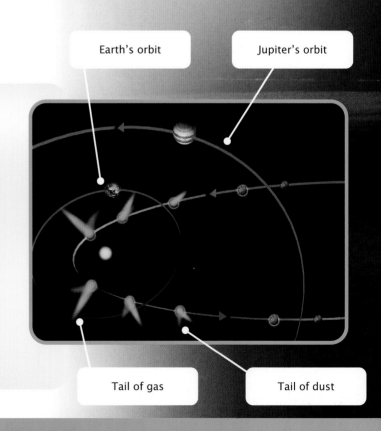

Earth's orbit

Jupiter's orbit

Tail of gas

Tail of dust

DID YOU KNOW? There are more than 4,580 known comets, but there are probably many more long-period comets currently in the far reaches of the Solar System.

The comet's faint, blue gas tail—containing high levels of super-hot carbon monoxide—stretched for hundreds of thousands of kilometers.

This golden tail was made of dust released from the nucleus, the grains reflecting the Sun's light.

The long-period comet Neowise was visible from Earth in 2020.

COMET NEOWISE PROFILE

Diameter of core: 5 km (3 miles)
Closest distance from the Sun: 43 million km (27 million miles)
Farthest distance from the Sun: 106 billion km (66 billion miles)
Orbit: Around 6,792 years
Named for: The WISE (Wide-Field Infrared Survey Explorer) telescope, through which astronomers first spotted the comet in 2020

Meteor Showers

Also known as a shooting star, a meteor is a glowing fragment of space rock that is falling through Earth's atmosphere. When many meteors appear from one point in the night sky, it is known as a meteor shower. Showers are caused by dust from a comet's tail or an asteroid.

The Geminids meteor shower appears to come from the direction of the Gemini star constellation.

Burning Up

Every day, millions of fragments from comets and asteroids enter Earth's atmosphere. These fragments crash into air molecules again and again, which makes them very hot—and creates a streak of light. Meteors become visible between 75 to 120 km (47 to 75 miles) above Earth's surface. Since most fragments are smaller than a grain of sand, they burn up completely before reaching Earth's surface, the majority of them without being noticed.

If a space rock is large enough to reach Earth's surface without burning up, it is known as a meteorite. This iron–rich meteorite fell in Russia in 1947.

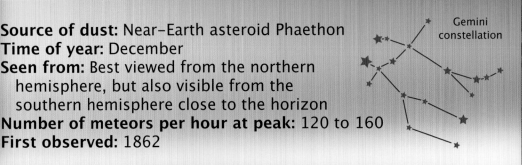

GEMINIDS SHOWER PROFILE	
Source of dust: Near–Earth asteroid Phaethon	
Time of year: December	
Seen from: Best viewed from the northern hemisphere, but also visible from the southern hemisphere close to the horizon	
Number of meteors per hour at peak: 120 to 160	
First observed: 1862	

Gemini constellation

DID YOU KNOW? The first written record of the Perseids meteor shower dates from the year 36, when it was observed over China.

This photo was taken with a long camera exposure, so it shows the night sky over several minutes.

Geminid meteors travel at 35 km/s (22 miles per second) and disintegrate at heights above 39 km (24 miles) from Earth's surface.

Yearly Events

Earth's year-long orbit takes it through the dust from several comet tails and disintegrating asteroids. This results in a series of meteor showers that take place at particular times of year, including the Lyrids in April, Leonids in November, and Ursids in December. Showers are named after the star constellation that lies in the direction from which they fall.

The Perseids meteor shower is caused by dust from the comet Swift–Tuttle and appears from the direction of the Perseus constellation in August. At the shower's peak, one meteor can be seen per minute, shown here in a long camera exposure.

Near-Earth Objects

A near-Earth object (NEO) is an asteroid, comet, or other small object that comes within 194 million km (120 million miles) of the Sun. If an NEO crosses Earth's orbit and is wider than 140 m (460 ft), it is considered a potentially hazardous object (PHO), so astronomers keep watch on it.

Around 170 m (560 ft) across, Dimorphos is a moon of near–Earth asteroid Didymos.

Staying Safe

Around 66 million years ago, an asteroid 10 km (6.2 miles) wide crashed into Earth, creating huge ocean waves and a cloud of dust that blocked out sunlight for a year. This impact wiped out the dinosaurs. Today, astronomers are working to prevent such a catastrophe happening again. In 2022, the *DART* (Double Asteroid Redirection Test) space probe was flown into the asteroid moon Dimorphos to change its orbit. This test helped astronomers calculate how to defend Earth against an approaching asteroid.

Astronomers and engineers celebrate the successful impact of *DART* with Dimorphos.

At 7 km (4 miles) wide, asteroid 1999 JM8 is the largest PHO. It passed 4.9 million km (3 million miles) from Earth in 1990, but on its next close approach, in 2075, it will be 38.3 million km (23.8 million miles) away. These images of the asteroid were created by the US space agency NASA (National Aeronautics and Space Administration).

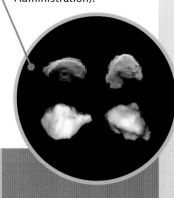

Danger in Numbers

Although most asteroids orbit in the Asteroid Belt, they can be knocked out of the belt by Jupiter's gravity, by passing close to Mars, or by an encounter with another object—allowing their orbit to near Earth. There are more than 29,000 known near-Earth asteroids and just 100 known near-Earth comets. Of all those NEOs, only 2,270 are considered PHOs. Only 17 of these PHOs will pass within 7.5 million km (4.6 million km) of Earth in the next 100 years. Nothing is currently on a collision course with Earth.

DIDYMOS PROFILE

Diameter: Up to 838 m (2,749 ft)
Mass: 0.00000000000008 Earths
Closest approach to Earth: 7.18 million km
(4.46 million miles) in 2003
Orbit around the Sun: 2.1 years
Rotation: 2.2 hours
Moons: 1 known

Didymos is a potentially hazardous object that will pass within 5.9 million km (3.7 million miles) of Earth in 2123.

This illustration pictures the *DART* probe as it hurtled toward Dimorphos at 24,000 km/h (15,000 miles per hour).

DID YOU KNOW? Earth's largest impact crater, Vredefort in South Africa, was 300 km (186 miles) wide when it was made by an asteroid around 2 billion years ago.

Farthest Regions

Beyond the Scattered Disk may lie two other groups of cold, distant, and mysterious objects: the detached objects and the even more distant Oort Cloud. Despite their vast distances from our star, these objects are still held in orbit by the Sun's immense gravity.

Detached Objects

These objects are too far away to be affected by the outer planets' gravity—making them appear "detached" from the rest of the Solar System. The few detached objects discovered so far have extremely elliptical orbits, which may have been affected by the pull of a passing star. The largest known detached object is the dwarf planet Sedna. When closest to the Sun (as it is now), Sedna is within the Scattered Disk, but at its most distant it is 140 billion km (87 billion miles) away.

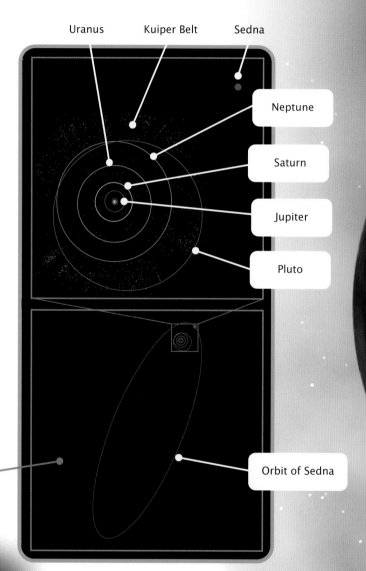

Uranus Kuiper Belt Sedna

Neptune

Saturn

Jupiter

Pluto

Orbit of Sedna

This diagram shows the orbit of Sedna compared with the orbits of the outer planets and Pluto.

SEDNA PROFILE

Diameter: Around 1,000 km (620 miles)
Mass: Not known
Average distance from the Sun:
    75.7 billion km (47 billion miles)
Orbit: Around 11,390 years
Rotation: Around 10 hours
Moons: None yet found

This illustration shows Sedna, which was discovered in 2003 and has not yet been photographed up close by a space probe.

It is not known if Sedna has a moon, but if not it would be the largest dwarf planet without one.

Oort Cloud

The existence of the Oort Cloud has not yet been proven, but it is believed to be a cloud of perhaps trillions of icy objects. Its existence was suggested by Dutch astronomer Jan Oort in 1950. The cloud is in interstellar space, beyond the bubble blown by the solar wind known as the heliosphere. The Oort Cloud objects may be the remains of material from the edge of the Sun's protoplanetary disk—which was then scattered by nearby stars and gas clouds.

The inner Oort Cloud may be ring-shaped, while the outer Oort Cloud may be a sphere that is more weakly bound by the Sun's gravity.

Telescope observations reveal that Sedna has a very red surface, which is probably composed of frozen water and methane that has been reddened by sunlight, like the methane on Pluto.

DID YOU KNOW? With our current technology, it would take a space probe 300 years to reach the inner edge of the Oort Cloud, perhaps 300 billion km (186 billion miles) away.

Chapter 6
Exploring the Solar System

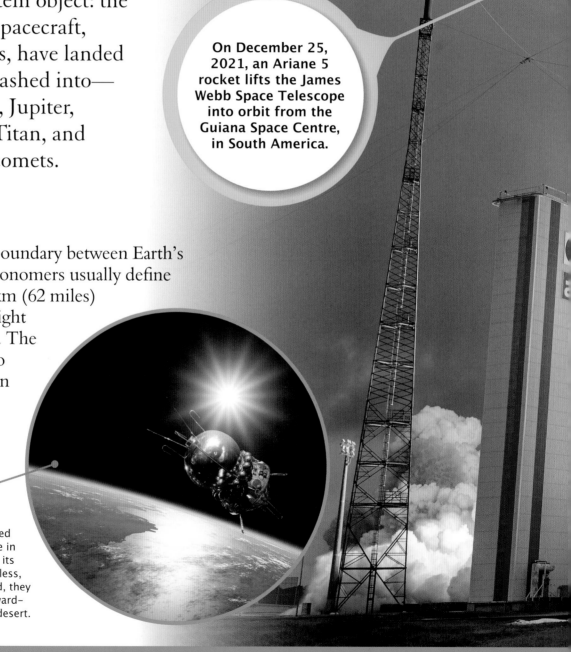

Apart from Earth, humans have walked on only one Solar System object: the Moon. Yet uncrewed spacecraft, known as space probes, have landed on—or deliberately crashed into—Mercury, Venus, Mars, Jupiter, Saturn and its moon Titan, and several asteroids and comets.

On December 25, 2021, an Ariane 5 rocket lifts the James Webb Space Telescope into orbit from the Guiana Space Centre, in South America.

Reaching Space

Since there is no definite boundary between Earth's atmosphere and space, astronomers usually define space as beginning at 100 km (62 miles) above Earth's surface, a height known as the Kármán line. The first human-made object to cross the line was a German V-2 rocket in 1944. The first human in space was the Soviet Union's Yuri Gagarin, in 1961.

Yuri Gagarin orbited Earth in the *Vostok 1* space capsule. Most crewed spacecraft have been capsules. Once in space, a capsule is steered by firing its engines. Yet, since capsules are wingless, they cannot glide back to Earth. Instead, they fall—slowed by a parachute or downward-blasting engines—landing in ocean or desert.

DID YOU KNOW? Until 1978, the only astronauts were from the Soviet Union and United States, but since then more than 500 people from over 40 countries have visited space.

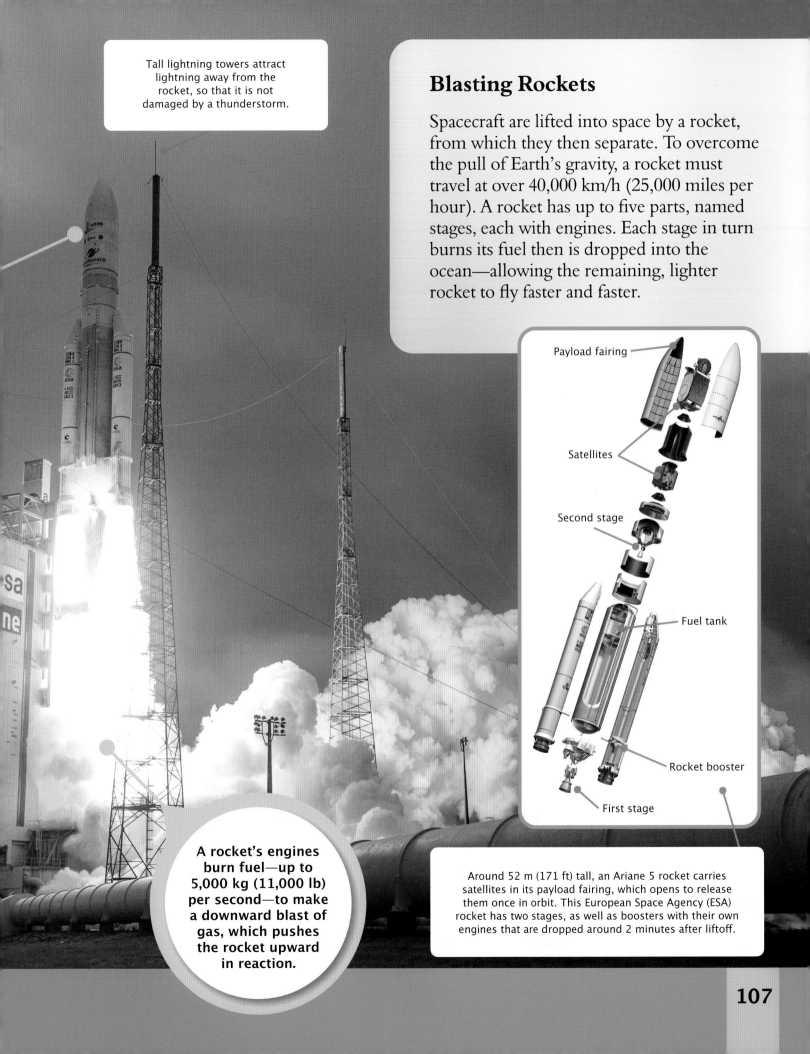

Tall lightning towers attract lightning away from the rocket, so that it is not damaged by a thunderstorm.

Blasting Rockets

Spacecraft are lifted into space by a rocket, from which they then separate. To overcome the pull of Earth's gravity, a rocket must travel at over 40,000 km/h (25,000 miles per hour). A rocket has up to five parts, named stages, each with engines. Each stage in turn burns its fuel then is dropped into the ocean—allowing the remaining, lighter rocket to fly faster and faster.

Payload fairing

Satellites

Second stage

Fuel tank

Rocket booster

First stage

A rocket's engines burn fuel—up to 5,000 kg (11,000 lb) per second—to make a downward blast of gas, which pushes the rocket upward in reaction.

Around 52 m (171 ft) tall, an Ariane 5 rocket carries satellites in its payload fairing, which opens to release them once in orbit. This European Space Agency (ESA) rocket has two stages, as well as boosters with their own engines that are dropped around 2 minutes after liftoff.

Going into Orbit

There are currently more than 5,000 satellites in orbit around Earth. From this high vantage point, satellites can help with communications on Earth or—equipped with telescopes, cameras, and sensors—have an unobstructed view of Earth, the Solar System, and beyond.

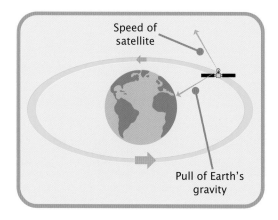

Speed of satellite

Pull of Earth's gravity

Staying Up

Satellites do not fall to Earth because the pull of Earth's gravity is balanced by the speed at which the satellite is moving away from Earth. A satellite does not need fuel to maintain this speed: It is given its speed by the rocket that lifts it into orbit and, since there is little to slow it down, it continues to move at much the same speed.

MEO
LEO
GEO

Common Orbits

Satellites with different purposes orbit at different heights above Earth. Those orbiting closer to Earth must travel faster to resist the stronger gravity.

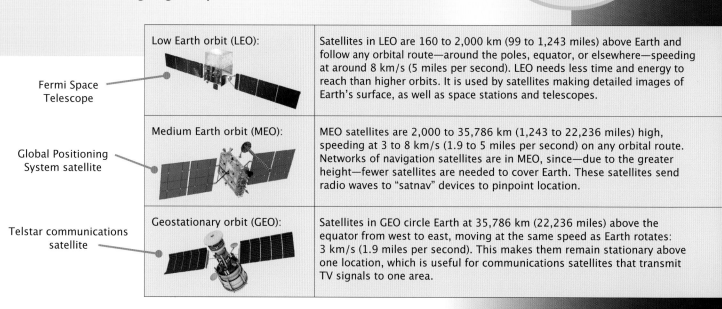

Fermi Space Telescope	**Low Earth orbit (LEO):**	Satellites in LEO are 160 to 2,000 km (99 to 1,243 miles) above Earth and follow any orbital route—around the poles, equator, or elsewhere—speeding at around 8 km/s (5 miles per second). LEO needs less time and energy to reach than higher orbits. It is used by satellites making detailed images of Earth's surface, as well as space stations and telescopes.
Global Positioning System satellite	**Medium Earth orbit (MEO):**	MEO satellites are 2,000 to 35,786 km (1,243 to 22,236 miles) high, speeding at 3 to 8 km/s (1.9 to 5 miles per second) on any orbital route. Networks of navigation satellites are in MEO, since—due to the greater height—fewer satellites are needed to cover Earth. These satellites send radio waves to "satnav" devices to pinpoint location.
Telstar communications satellite	**Geostationary orbit (GEO):**	Satellites in GEO circle Earth at 35,786 km (22,236 miles) above the equator from west to east, moving at the same speed as Earth rotates: 3 km/s (1.9 miles per second). This makes them remain stationary above one location, which is useful for communications satellites that transmit TV signals to one area.

From low Earth orbit, the Hubble Space Telescope has a view of the Solar System that is not distorted by Earth's atmosphere or city lights.

This door closes when Hubble points toward the Sun, to prevent light from flooding its cameras. These observe visible, ultraviolet, and infrared light with the help of a 2.4-m (7.9-ft) wide mirror to gather light.

Solar panels absorb sunlight, which is turned into electricity to power the telescope's equipment.

HUBBLE SPACE TELESCOPE PROFILE

Size: 13.2 m (43 ft) long and 4.2 m (14 ft) wide
Mass: 12,000 kg (27,000 lb)
Average height above Earth: 540 km (336 miles)
Orbit around Earth: 95 minutes
Launched: 1990
Named after: American astronomer Edwin Hubble, who proved in 1924 that there were galaxies beyond the Milky Way

DID YOU KNOW? The first satellite to orbit Earth was the Soviet Union's *Sputnik 1*, which managed to stay in orbit from October 1957 to January 1958.

International Space Station

The International Space Station (ISS) is shared by Canada, Europe, Japan, Russia, and the United States. A space station is a satellite with room for human crew. The ISS was not the first and is not the only station in Earth orbit, but it is the largest and has been occupied for longest.

Going Farther

The ISS crew conducts experiments that will help us continue human exploration of the Solar System safely. The astronauts monitor themselves to see how their body is responding to being in a low-gravity environment for many weeks or months. Plant experiments give ideas about how astronauts might feed themselves on a long-term space mission.

Solar panel

Astronaut Stephanie Wilson and her equipment appear to float aboard the ISS as they are all in free fall (falling in a curving path; see page 108) around Earth.

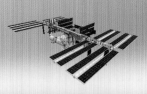

ISS PROFILE

Size: 73 m (239 ft) long and 109 m (358 ft) wide
Average height above Earth: 408 km (254 miles)
Orbit around Earth: 93 minutes
Launched: 1998
Inhabited: Since 2000
Crew: 7

DID YOU KNOW? Launched in 2021, China's Tiangong (meaning "Heavenly Palace" in Chinese) Space Station has a rotating crew of six astronauts.

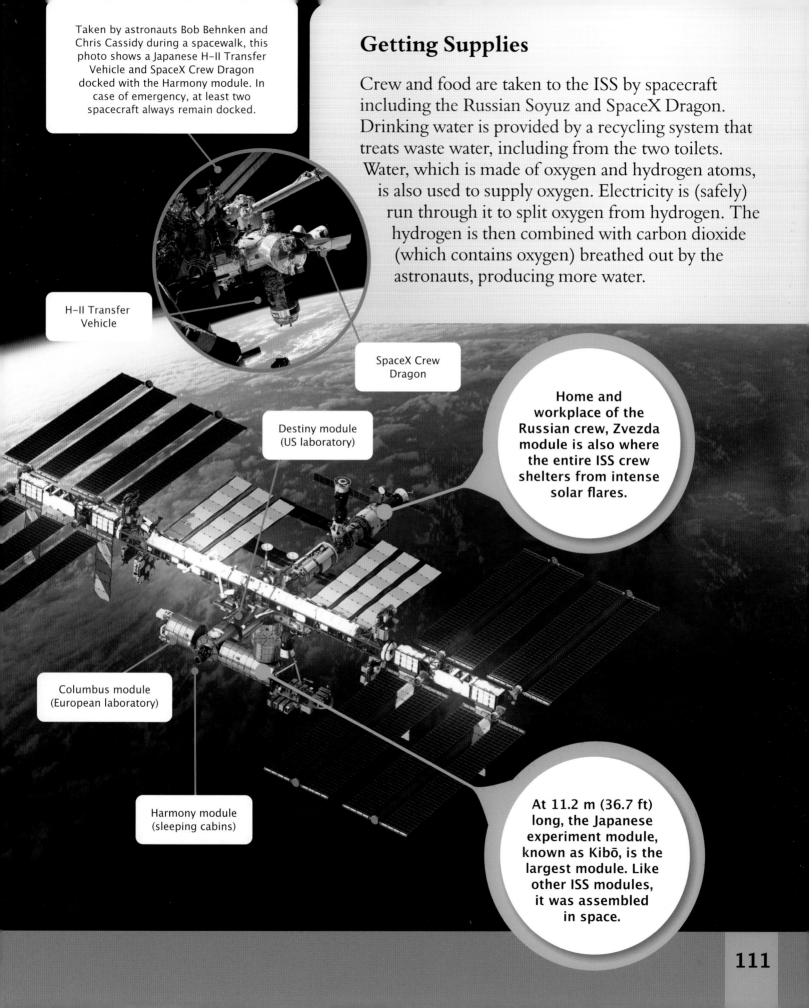

Taken by astronauts Bob Behnken and Chris Cassidy during a spacewalk, this photo shows a Japanese H–II Transfer Vehicle and SpaceX Crew Dragon docked with the Harmony module. In case of emergency, at least two spacecraft always remain docked.

Getting Supplies

Crew and food are taken to the ISS by spacecraft including the Russian Soyuz and SpaceX Dragon. Drinking water is provided by a recycling system that treats waste water, including from the two toilets. Water, which is made of oxygen and hydrogen atoms, is also used to supply oxygen. Electricity is (safely) run through it to split oxygen from hydrogen. The hydrogen is then combined with carbon dioxide (which contains oxygen) breathed out by the astronauts, producing more water.

H–II Transfer Vehicle

SpaceX Crew Dragon

Destiny module (US laboratory)

Home and workplace of the Russian crew, Zvezda module is also where the entire ISS crew shelters from intense solar flares.

Columbus module (European laboratory)

Harmony module (sleeping cabins)

At 11.2 m (36.7 ft) long, the Japanese experiment module, known as Kibō, is the largest module. Like other ISS modules, it was assembled in space.

Landing on the Moon

The greatest breakthrough in space exploration came on July 20, 1969, when the first humans walked on the Moon: Neil Armstrong and Edwin "Buzz" Aldrin. Since then, only 10 other people have walked there, the last in 1972.

Apollo 11

The mission that landed the first humans on the Moon was the United States' Apollo 11. The Apollo spacecraft had three parts: a command module (with living quarters) and service module (with engines and supplies), which were together known as *Columbia*; and a lunar module, known as *Eagle*.

Since there is no wind on the Moon, the US flag was fitted with a horizontal bar so it would not hang limp in photos of the Moon landing.

The Apollo spacecraft was launched by a Saturn V rocket on July 16, 1969.

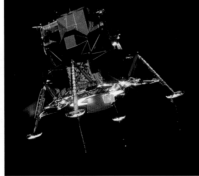

After entering Moon orbit, Armstrong and Aldrin flew *Eagle* (pictured) down to the Moon's surface, while pilot Michael Collins remained alone aboard *Columbia*, from where he took this photo.

The command module holding the astronauts was the only spacecraft portion intended to return to Earth, which it did on July 24, in the Pacific Ocean.

Robot Visitors

A rover is a robotic space probe that travels across the surface of a space object. The first lunar rover—and the first successful rover on any space object—was the Soviet Union's *Lunokhod 1* in 1970. The first rover to operate on the Moon's far side was China's *Yutu-2*, in 2019. *Yutu-2* has solar panels to supply power, as well as a heater that uses radioactivity (the decay of unstable atoms) to warm it during the long, cold nights.

This photo of *Yutu-2* was taken by its lander *Chang'e 4*, which extended a ramp for the rover to roll onto the surface. *Yutu-2* uses radio waves to send information back to Earth.

During the Apollo 11 mission, Armstrong and Aldrin loaded 21.5 kg (47.5 lb) of lunar rocks and dust onto *Eagle*.

This is one of the few photos of Neil Armstrong on the Moon, since he took most of the photos, showing Aldrin. Armstrong was the first to step out of *Eagle*, saying: "That's one small step for [a] man, one giant leap for mankind."

COLUMBIA PROFILE

Size: 11 m (36.2 ft) long and up to 3.9 m (12.8 ft) wide
Mass at launch: 28,000 kg (62,000 lb)
Volume: 6.2 cu m (218 cu ft)
Engines: 1 AJ10 rocket engine
Design in use: 1966 to 1975
Crew: 3

DID YOU KNOW? There was no toilet on the Apollo 11 spacecraft, so the astronauts peed and pooped in bags that were taken back to Earth.

Studying the Sun

Satellites with special cameras and equipment, known as solar observatories, are monitoring the Sun. Due to the Sun's temperature and lack of a solid surface, it is not possible for a probe to land—but in 2021, a probe "touched" the Sun for the first time.

Touching the Sun

In April 2021, the *Parker Solar Probe* was the first probe to orbit through the Sun's corona, touching its upper atmosphere, around 13 million km (8.1 million miles) above the "surface." The probe sampled solar wind particles and magnetic fields. On *Parker*'s even closer approaches to the surface, of around 6.16 million km (3.83 million miles), the Sun's gravity accelerated the probe's speed to 690,000 km/h (430,000 miles per hour), making it the fastest object ever built.

The *Parker Solar Probe* has a solar shield—made of the engineered material "carbon reinforced with carbon"—that can withstand temperatures of 1,370 °C (2,500 °F), keeping its instruments at around 30 °C (85 °F).

The *Solar and Heliospheric Observatory (SOHO)* studies the Sun's interior by observing vibrations on its surface, a technique known as helioseismology.

Orbiting the Sun

Launched in 2021, *Solar Orbiter (SolO)* is currently the closest probe to the Sun with a camera, 42 million km (26 million miles) away at its nearest. It orbits the Sun rather than Earth, having reached that orbit with help from the Sun's pull and through gravity assists from Earth and Venus. A gravity assist, also known as a slingshot, is when a spacecraft uses the movement and gravity of a planet or moon to alter its path and speed, in order to save fuel on its long journey.

These images of the Sun's surface materials were taken by *SolO* using different wavelengths of ultraviolet light. Clockwise from top left, they show: hydrogen, carbon, neon, and oxygen.

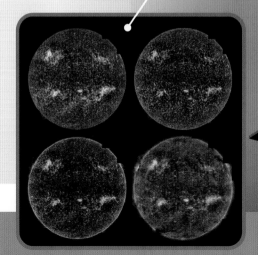

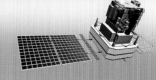

SOHO PROFILE

Size: 4.3 m (14 ft) long and 3.7 m (12 ft) wide
Mass: 610 kg (1,340 lb)
Average distance from Earth: 1.5 million km (932,000 miles)
Average distance from the Sun: 148 million km (92 million miles)
Orbit: 6 months around Lagrange point; 1 year around the Sun
Launched: 1995

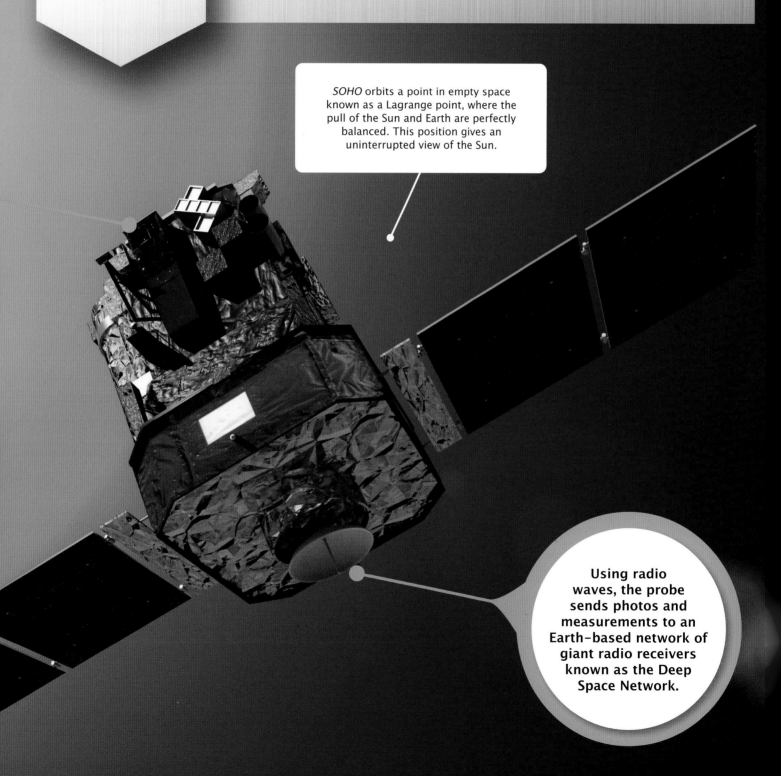

SOHO orbits a point in empty space known as a Lagrange point, where the pull of the Sun and Earth are perfectly balanced. This position gives an uninterrupted view of the Sun.

Using radio waves, the probe sends photos and measurements to an Earth-based network of giant radio receivers known as the Deep Space Network.

DID YOU KNOW? The first probe to orbit the Sun was *Luna 1*, which in 1959 missed its target of the Moon and sailed into an orbit between Earth and Mars.

Missions to Mars

Apart from Earth and the Moon, Mars is the most explored object in the Solar System. Mars has been successfully visited by 6 rovers, more than 10 landers (which land on the surface and survey one spot), and 18 orbiters (which monitor the planet and atmosphere from orbit).

Researching Rovers

Mars is the only planet to which we have sent rovers. The Mars rover *Sojourner* was the first wheeled vehicle to travel on a planet other than Earth, in 1997. Rovers use drills, lasers, and testing equipment such as X-ray tubes to study the chemicals in Martian rocks, searching particularly for signs of water or life. Rovers contain computers that are programmed to perform some tasks independently, but other instructions are received from Earth by radio waves.

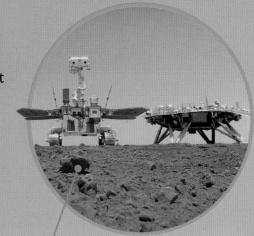

In 2021, China's Mars rover *Zhurong* took this selfie beside its lander using a remote-controlled camera.

NASA's *Perseverance* rover has 19 cameras and 2 microphones.

DID YOU KNOW? In April 2021, *Perseverance* became the first spacecraft to record the noise of another spacecraft, *Ingenuity*, on another planet.

Perseverance is supported by the helicopter *Ingenuity*, which looks for areas of possible interest for the rover to explore.

Humans on Mars

Several national space agencies, including the United States' NASA and Russia's Roscosmos, have plans to send humans to Mars within 30 years, possibly to set up a base on the planet or in orbit. With current spacecraft technology, and taking advantage of the best positions of the planets in their orbits, the shortest trip would be a 9-month journey from Earth to Mars, about 16 months on Mars to wait for the right moment to return, then a 9-month journey home.

NASA is developing a spacecraft, Deep Space Transport, large enough for a crew of six as they rest and exercise on a journey to Mars. It is based on NASA's Orion space capsule, first tested in 2014, attached to a Deep Space Habitat.

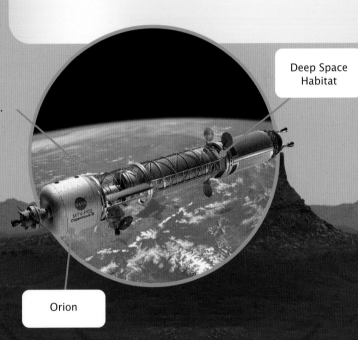

Deep Space Habitat

Orion

No lander has yet taken off from Mars, but *Perseverance* is collecting tubes of samples that will be picked up by a future lander–rover mission.

PERSEVERANCE PROFILE

Size: 2.9 m (9.5 ft) long and 2.2 m (7.2 ft) wide
Mass: 1,025 kg (2,260 lb)
Location: Jezero Crater, Mars
Landed on Mars: 2021
Carried to Mars by: *Mars 2020* spacecraft
Launched from Earth by: Atlas V rocket

Mars 2020 spacecraft

Cruise stage

Protective backshell

Descent stage

Perseverance and *Ingenuity*

Heat shield

Mapping the Inferior Planets

Mercury and Venus are known as the inferior planets because they are closer to the Sun than Earth. Due to the intense heat of these planets, no rover has journeyed on either, but probes have sent us images and information that let us map their cratered surfaces.

> Two square solar panels, 2.5 m (8.2 ft) across, made electricity from sunlight and charged batteries that were used for power when *Magellan* was in shadow.

Meeting Mercury

Mercury is the least explored inner planet because of its closeness to the Sun. Mercury orbits the Sun so quickly that a spacecraft must travel very fast to meet it. The intense gravity of the nearby Sun means that a spacecraft then has to brake very hard to enter orbit around Mercury. The first probe to orbit Mercury was *MESSENGER*, from 2011 to 2015. It was the second mission to near the planet, after *Mariner 10*, which flew past Mercury three times in 1974–75, passing 327 km (203 miles) away while orbiting the Sun.

MESSENGER became the first human–made object on the surface of Mercury when it was allowed to crash into the planet at the end of its mission.

MAGELLAN PROFILE

Size: 6.4 m (21 ft) long and 4.6 m (15 ft) wide
Mass: 1,035 kg (2,282 lb)
Average distance from Venus: 10,470 km (6,510 miles)
Launched: 1989
In orbit around Venus: 1990-94
Named after: Portuguese sailor Ferdinand Magellan, who led the first circumnavigation (journey around) Earth in 1519-22

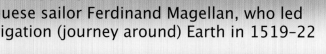

DID YOU KNOW? After missing Venusian orbit in 2010, Japanese probe *Akatsuki* orbited the Sun until it could enter Venus's orbit in 2015 by firing its thruster engines for 20 minutes.

Venus's clouds are opaque to visible light, but radio waves can pass through them, bounce off Venus's surface, then return to a probe.

Visiting Venus

Due to Venus's closeness to Earth, many probes have carried out flybys, orbits, and landings. The first successful interplanetary probe, *Mariner 2*, flew past Venus in 1962. The probe that spent longest in Venusian orbit was *Pioneer Venus*, which studied Venus's atmosphere from 1978 to 1992. Due to Venus's heat and the pressure of its atmosphere, the longest any lander has transmitted from Venus's surface is 127 minutes, the record held by *Venera 13*, in 1982.

As *Magellan* orbited Venus, the probe used a large antenna to send out radio waves that mapped 95 percent of the planet's surface.

The Soviet Union's *Venera 13* lander recorded sounds and took photos, which were transmitted to its orbiter, which relayed them to Earth.

Watching the Giant Planets

No probe can land on the giant planets due to their lack of a solid surface, but nine probes have orbited or flown past at least one of them. All nine of these probes visited Jupiter, four also passed or orbited Saturn—and just one went on to fly past Uranus and Neptune.

Three Orbiters

Only three probes have orbited one of the giant planets. From 1995 to 2003, *Galileo* orbited Jupiter, discovering the planet's rings are made of dust from the inner moons. Having performed a gravity assist (see page 114) around Jupiter, the *Cassini* probe orbited Saturn from 2004 to 2017, capturing photos of immense storms. *Juno* entered orbit around Jupiter in 2016.

In 1995, *Galileo* (right) dropped a probe (left) into Jupiter's atmosphere. The probe transmitted information—revealing thunderstorms larger than Earth—for 58 minutes, until it was crushed by Jupiter's pressure.

JUNO PROFILE

Size: 4.6 m (15 ft) long and 20.1 m (66 ft) wide
Mass: 1,593 kg (3,512 lb)
Average distance from Jupiter: 4 million km (2.5 million miles)
Launched: 2011
Entered orbit around Jupiter: 2016
Named after: Roman goddess Juno, wife of the god Jupiter, who alone was able to see Jupiter's true nature

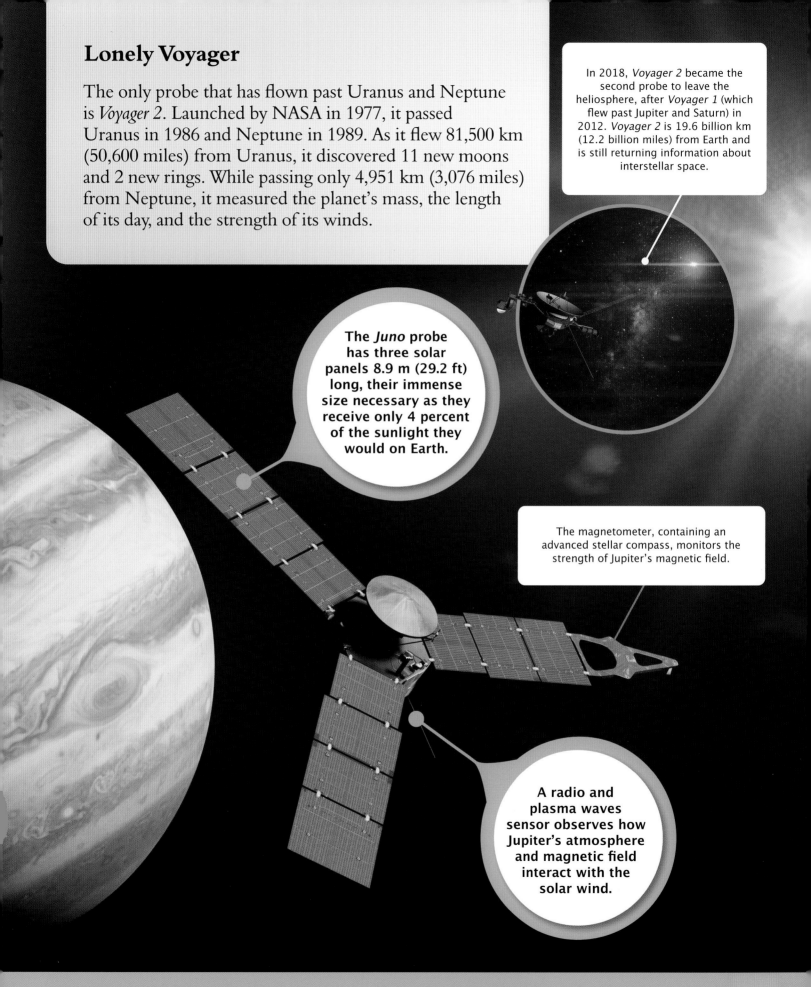

Lonely Voyager

The only probe that has flown past Uranus and Neptune is *Voyager 2*. Launched by NASA in 1977, it passed Uranus in 1986 and Neptune in 1989. As it flew 81,500 km (50,600 miles) from Uranus, it discovered 11 new moons and 2 new rings. While passing only 4,951 km (3,076 miles) from Neptune, it measured the planet's mass, the length of its day, and the strength of its winds.

In 2018, *Voyager 2* became the second probe to leave the heliosphere, after *Voyager 1* (which flew past Jupiter and Saturn) in 2012. *Voyager 2* is 19.6 billion km (12.2 billion miles) from Earth and is still returning information about interstellar space.

The *Juno* probe has three solar panels 8.9 m (29.2 ft) long, their immense size necessary as they receive only 4 percent of the sunlight they would on Earth.

The magnetometer, containing an advanced stellar compass, monitors the strength of Jupiter's magnetic field.

A radio and plasma waves sensor observes how Jupiter's atmosphere and magnetic field interact with the solar wind.

DID YOU KNOW? Probes that have visited the giant planets are *Pioneers 10* and *11*, *Voyagers 1* and *2*, *Galileo*, *Ulysses*, *Cassini*, *New Horizons*, and *Juno*.

Distant Moons

Only one moon apart from our own has been landed on: Titan, the largest moon of Saturn. However, other moons—belonging to Mars, Jupiter, and Saturn—have been flown past by probes that have taken photos and studied their motion, surface, and atmosphere.

This illustration shows *Huygens'* descent to Titan, at first protected by its heat shield, which reached 1,800 °C (3,270 °F) due to friction with the moon's atmosphere.

Touching Titan

Due to its nitrogen atmosphere a little like Earth's, Titan attracted astronomers hoping for signs of tiny life forms. During its orbits of Saturn, the *Cassini* probe flew close by Titan several times, on one occasion releasing a lander named *Huygens*, which touched down on the Moon in 2005. Although no signs of life were found, the *Cassini-Huygens* mission revealed that Titan has seas of methane and ethane, as well as a possible underground ocean of water and ammonia.

Huygens transmitted information and photos, including this one, for 90 minutes after touchdown. The rocks and pebbles are made of water ice.

HUYGENS PROFILE

Size: 1.3 m (4.3 ft) across
Mass: 320 kg (710 lb)
Location: Adiri region, Titan
Launched: 1997
Landed on Titan: 2005
Named after: Dutch astronomer Christiaan Huygens, who discovered Titan in 1655

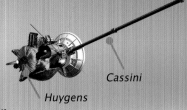

Cassini

Huygens

DID YOU KNOW? The European, Japanese, Russian, and US space agencies have plans to take rock samples from the Martian moon Phobos, then return them to Earth.

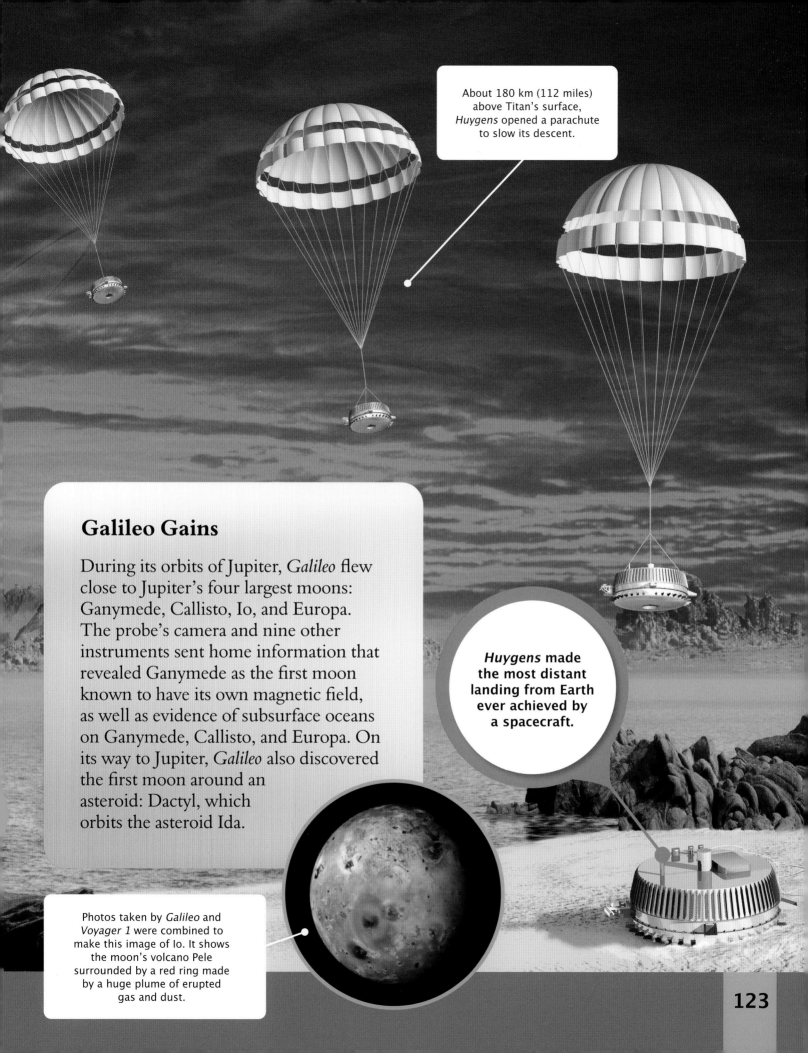

About 180 km (112 miles) above Titan's surface, *Huygens* opened a parachute to slow its descent.

Galileo Gains

During its orbits of Jupiter, *Galileo* flew close to Jupiter's four largest moons: Ganymede, Callisto, Io, and Europa. The probe's camera and nine other instruments sent home information that revealed Ganymede as the first moon known to have its own magnetic field, as well as evidence of subsurface oceans on Ganymede, Callisto, and Europa. On its way to Jupiter, *Galileo* also discovered the first moon around an asteroid: Dactyl, which orbits the asteroid Ida.

Huygens made the most distant landing from Earth ever achieved by a spacecraft.

Photos taken by *Galileo* and *Voyager 1* were combined to make this image of Io. It shows the moon's volcano Pele surrounded by a red ring made by a huge plume of erupted gas and dust.

Small Objects

More than 25 asteroids, comets, and Kuiper Belt objects have been visited by space probes. The largest of these objects was the biggest dwarf planet in the Kuiper Belt, Pluto, which was flown past by *New Horizons* in 2015. Among the smallest was the asteroid Itokawa, around 330 m (1,080 ft) across.

In 2005, the NASA probe *Deep Impact* released an impactor to study the interior of comet Tempel 1.

Catching Comets

A mission to the comet Wild 2 was the first to return a sample of material from a space object other than Earth's Moon. In 2004, the *Stardust* probe passed within 237 km (147 miles) of Wild 2 to collect dust flying from its nucleus. The dust landed on Earth in 2006 aboard *Stardust*'s sample-return capsule. Comets were not believed to get warm enough to melt their icy nucleus fully, but—unexpectedly—the particles showed signs of liquid water.

As Wild 2 overtook *Stardust* in their orbits round the Sun, dust flying from the comet's nucleus was collected in a grille filled with aerogel, a human-made, sponge-like material.

The impactor, a probe designed to dent a space object, made a crater on the comet around 100 m (328 ft) wide and 30 m (98 ft) deep.

DEEP IMPACT PROFILE

Size: 3.3 m (10.8 ft) long and 2.3 m (7.5 ft) wide
Mass of main probe: 601 kg (1,325 lb)
Mass of impactor: 372 kg (820 lb)
Meeting with Tempel 1: Around 230 million km (143 million miles) from the Sun
Distance from Tempel 1 of main probe: 575 km (357 miles)
Launched: 2005

DID YOU KNOW? In 2002, *Stardust* tested its flyby technique on the asteroid Annefrank, named after the Jewish teenage diary writer who died in the Holocaust in 1945.

Approaching Asteroids

Missions to asteroids are trying to learn more about the motions and materials of asteroids, since these leftovers offer clues about the formation of the Solar System. The first orbit of an asteroid, as well as the first landing, was made by *NEAR (Near Earth Asteroid Rendezvous) Shoemaker* on the near-Earth asteroid Eros, in 2000–2001. The first probe to collect dust from an asteroid was Japan's *Hayabusa*, which took material from Itokawa in 2005.

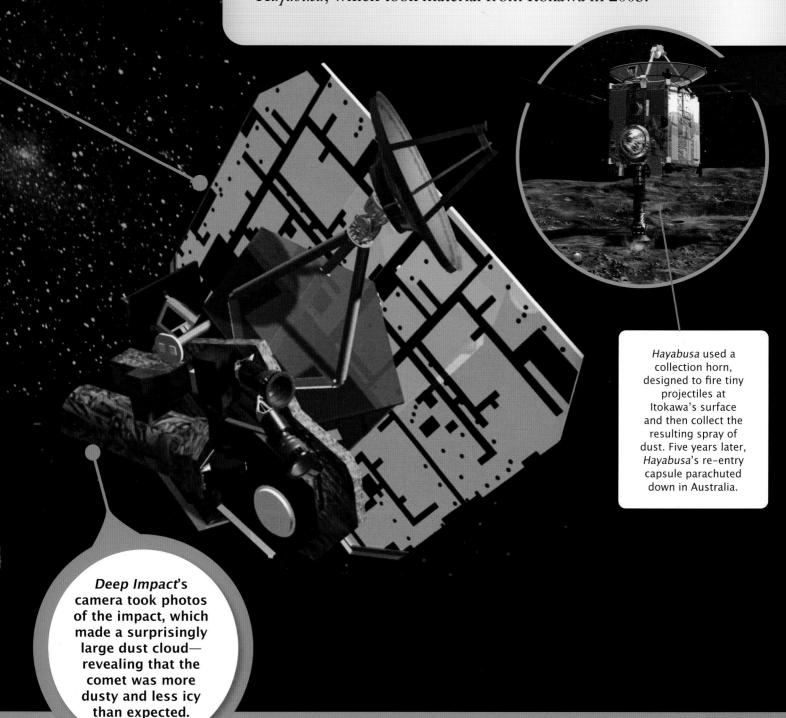

Hayabusa used a collection horn, designed to fire tiny projectiles at Itokawa's surface and then collect the resulting spray of dust. Five years later, *Hayabusa*'s re-entry capsule parachuted down in Australia.

Deep Impact's camera took photos of the impact, which made a surprisingly large dust cloud— revealing that the comet was more dusty and less icy than expected.

Glossary

ASTEROID
A small rocky or metal object that orbits the Sun.

ASTEROID BELT
A ring-shaped region, between the orbits of Mars and Jupiter, that contains many asteroids.

ASTRONOMER
A scientist who studies the planets, stars, and other objects in space.

ASTRONOMICAL UNIT (AU)
The average distance from Earth to the Sun: 150 million km (93 million miles).

ATMOSPHERE
The gases surrounding a planet or moon, held by its gravity.

ATOM
The smallest unit of matter. An atom has a central nucleus, containing particles called protons and neutrons, usually surrounded by one or more electrons.

AURORA
Lights in the sky made by particles from the Sun exciting gases in the atmosphere.

AXIS
An imaginary line through the middle of a planet or moon, around which the object rotates.

BLACK HOLE
An area of space with such strong gravity that no matter or light can escape from it.

CARBON DIOXIDE
A substance made of carbon and oxygen atoms; a gas at room temperature.

CENTAUR
A small icy object orbiting the Sun in the region of the outer planets.

CHROMOSPHERE
An inner layer of the Sun's atmosphere.

COMET
A small icy object with an elliptical orbit that takes it both close to and far from the Sun.

CONSTELLATION
A group of stars that seem to make a shape in the night sky.

CORE
The inner region of a planet or moon.

CORONA
The outer layer of the Sun's atmosphere.

CRUST
The outer layer of a planet or moon.

DENSE
Tightly packed.

DIAMETER
A straight line through the middle of a sphere.

DWARF PLANET
An object orbiting a star that is massive enough for its gravity to pull it into a ball, but is not massive enough to clear other objects out of its path.

ECLIPSE
When a body such as a star, planet, or moon is obscured by passing into the shadow of—or behind—another body.

ELECTRIC CHARGE
A property of electrons and protons. Electrons are negatively charged and protons are positively charged. Electricity is a flow of electrically charged particles.

ELECTRON
A particle found in atoms.

ELLIPTICAL
Shaped like a stretched circle.

ENERGY
The power to do work that produces light, heat, or motion.

EXOPLANET
A planet outside our Solar System.

FRICTION
The force that resists the movement of one object past another.

GALAXY
Millions of stars, as well as gas and dust, held together by gravity.

GAS
A substance, such as air, that can move freely and has no fixed shape.

GRAVITY
A force that pulls all objects and particles toward each other.

HELIOSPHERE
A bubble blown by the solar wind.

HELIUM
The second most common atom; a gas at room temperature.

HYDROGEN
The most common atom; a gas at room temperature.